THE CATHOLIC UNIVERSITY OF AMERICA
CANON LAW STUDIES
No. 158

THE PRECEPT OF HEARING MASS

A HISTORICAL CONSPECTUS AND COMMENTARY

by

JOHN JOSEPH GUINIVEN, C.SS.R., J.C.L.
Priest of the Baltimore Province

A DISSERTATION

Submitted to the Faculty of Canon Law of the Catholic University of America in Partial Fulfillment of the Requirements for the Degree of Doctor of Canon Law

THE CATHOLIC UNIVERSITY OF AMERICA PRESS
WASHINGTON, D. C.
1942

Imprimi Potest:

GULIELMUS T. MCCARTY, C.SS.R.,

Superior Provincialis.

Brooklynii, die 1 iunii 1942.

Nihil Obstat:

CLEMENS V. BASTNAGEL, J.U.D., S.T.L.,

Censor Deputatus.

Washingtonii, D. C., die 29 maii 1942.

Imprimatur:

✠ MICHAEL J. CURLEY, D.D.,

Archiepiscopus Baltimorensis.

Baltimorae, Md., die 29 maii 1942.

Printed by
THE PAULIST PRESS
New York, N Y
51

TO

THE MOST HOLY REDEEMER

OUR MOTHER OF PERPETUAL HELP

AND

ST. ALPHONSUS

TABLE OF CONTENTS

CHAPTER III

CHAPTER IV

CHAPTER V

CHAPTER VIII

CHAPTER IX

INTRODUCTION

THE purpose of this study is twofold: to trace the development of the precept of hearing Mass on Sundays and Feastdays from its origin down to the adoption of the New Code of Canon Law, and to offer an interpretation of the ecclesiastical discipline regarding this precept as it exists today. The selection of this topic was prompted by the conviction that the precept of hearing Mass is of sufficient importance to merit special and exclusive consideration. Most of the works dealing with it consider it only as part of the more general precept of sanctifying Sundays and Feastdays, which includes the concomitant obligation of abstaining from servile work. Almost without exception these works devote more consideration to the latter negative aspect of Sunday and Feastday observance—a procedure necessitated no doubt by the confusion and uncertainty attending it. Furthermore, even those treatises which deal exclusively with the precept of attending Mass on Sundays and Feastdays leave much to be desired in the matter of a thorough investigation of the subject as extending from its origin down to and including the legislation of the New Code.

The obligation incumbent upon Catholics to hear Mass constitutes the more important aspect of their general obligation to sanctify Sundays and Feastdays. The less important aspect, namely, the mere abstention from servile work and worldly pursuits, does not in itself offer much by way of contribution to the required sanctification of the days in question. It is rather a condition which makes it possible for the faithful to achieve the sanctification of these days by a fuller devotion of themselves to prayer and worship. Attendance at Mass, on the other hand, is the greatest act of worship which the faithful can offer to God, and the greatest source of blessings contributing to their own personal sanctification. The Sacrifice of the Mass is the center around which Christian life revolves, and the most perfect expression of the worship which Christians, as members of the Mystical Body of Christ, owe their God and Creator. To quote Ellard, in his comparison of the Mass with the sacrifice of Christ on Calvary:

> On the Cross, although acting on behalf of all mankind, Christ necessarily acted *alone;* in the Mass, while still acting on behalf of all men, Christ sacrifices *with* His whole Mystical Body. Nay, more: in the Mass Christ sacrifices only *through* His Mystical Body, only as conditioned by the Mystical Body. That is to say, unless the Mystical Body "does this in memory of Him," the great High Priest Himself must remain inactive.[1]

Certainly then, the Sacrifice of the Mass is of supreme importance in the economy of Christian life. And the obligation imposed by the Church upon every Christian of assisting at stated times at this Sacrifice is consequently of sufficient importance to deserve the special consideration which this study attempts to give it.

A thorough investigation of this matter demands of necessity that the writer make lengthy excursions into the field of moral theology. It is his purpose, however, to provide a study of the precept of hearing Mass under all its varied aspects, and therefore the consideration of matters which pertain to moral theology rather than to Canon Law is not only justified but necessary.

The writer is pleased to discharge a great debt of gratitude by expressing his thanks and appreciation to his Very Reverend Provincial, William T. McCarty, C.SS.R., for the opportunity to complete his advanced studies in Canon Law; to the faculty of the School of Canon Law of the Catholic University for their profitable instruction and generous assistance, and especially to the Rev. Clement V. Bastnagel, J.U.D., for his painstaking and invaluable direction and help in the preparation of this dissertation. The writer expresses his gratitude also to his confreres for their interest and aid and encouragement; to the librarians of the Catholic University for their cheerful and capable co-operation; and finally, to those to whom this dissertation is dedicated, for help and encouragement without which this dissertation, and the course of advanced studies, would never have been completed.

[1] Ellard, *Christian Life and Worship* (Milwaukee: Bruce Publishing Company, 1933), p. 186.

Part One

Historical Synopsis

CHAPTER I

JEWISH OBSERVANCE OF THE SABBATH AND FEASTDAYS

Article I. Relation of the Jewish to the Christian Observance

Before one traces the development of the Sunday and Feastday observance in the Catholic Church, it is fitting that one examine the corresponding observance in the Old Testament, namely, the Sabbath and Feastday observance of the Jewish religion. This procedure will be profitable because

(a) the same basic reasons underlay the Jewish observance;
(b) the Jewish observance foreshadowed the observance of the Catholic Church;
(c) the Jewish observance was, in part, actually adopted by the Catholic Church.

(a) Same Basic Reasons Underlying Both

The Sabbath and Feastday observance of the Jews was twofold: namely, rest from work, and devotion to prayer and worship. The purpose of this twofold observance was to enable the Jews to turn away from themselves, and to devote themselves fully to God. This is indicated in the words of Isaias:

> If thou turn away . . . from doing thy own will in my holy day . . . and glorify Him, while thou dost not thy own ways . . . then shalt thou be delighted in the Lord. . . .[1]

[1] Isaias lviii. 13-14.

The Sabbath-rest was observed to commemorate the rest of God Himself on the seventh day of creation,[2] and also, at a later period, to remind His people of their deliverance from Egypt, which, giving them as it did a new existence as a free people, was in a certain sense a new creation.[3] This in turn lifted their minds toward the God Who had created them, and Who would sanctify them.[4]

The mere cessation from labor, the negative element of the observance, even though it was observed in commemoration of the rest of God the Creator, hardly served in a direct way to sanctify the Sabbath. And so it was the positive element, prayer and worship, which constituted the chief means of fulfilling the command of God to sanctify His holy day.[5] This is expressed by the prayer contained in the so-called Apostolic Constitutions: " . . . Thou didst command them, the Jews, to keep the Sabbath, not that it might be unto them an occasion of idleness, but a help unto godliness. . . ."[6]

(b) Jewish Observance Foreshadowed Christian

The Old Testament abounds in types or figures which foreshadow persons, events or things of the New Dispensation. While the Sabbath and Feastdays of the Jews were not, in the strict sense of the word, types of the Sunday and Feastdays of the Christians, there exists nevertheless a striking resemblance between them. The Sabbath and Jewish Feastdays, characterized as they were by abstention from work and by devotion to prayer and worship, mirror the Sunday and Feastdays of the Christian religion, which even to the present day are observed in a similar manner. The words of St. Paul bear out this statement: "Let no man therefore judge you . . . in respect of a festival day, or of the new moon, or of the sabbaths, which are a shadow of things to come . . ."[7] St. Caesarius

[2] Exodus xxxi. 17; Deuteronomy v. 14.

[3] Deuteronomy v. 15.

[4] Exodus xxi. 13; Ezechiel xx. 12.

[5] Deuteronomy v. 12; Exodus xvi. 23; Jeremias xvii. 22.

[6] Funk, *Didascalia et Constitutiones Apostolorum* (2 vols., Paderbornae, 1905), I, 435.

[7] Colossians ii. 16-17.

of Arles expresses the same idea, when he says that the holy doctors of the Church wished all the glory of the Jewish sabbath to be transferred to Sunday, so that what the Jews celebrated in figure, we may celebrate in truth.[8] So also the II Council of Macon (585) says that "Sunday is the perpetual day of rest foreshadowed in the seventh day and made known to us in the law and the Prophets." [9]

This resemblance is especially apparent in the sphere of worship generally,[10] but extends also to the seriousness of the obligation, because among the Jews the violation of the observance, just as among the Christians, constituted a grave sin, and was punished by the most severe penalties.[11] The gravity of this obligation, as that of the Christian, was based not on the fact that the violation was in itself anything serious, but because in that violation was implied a denial to God of the honor and recognition due to Him. It was a factual negation of what the Sabbath signified.

Another point of similarity between the Jewish Sabbath and the Christian Sunday, and between the respective Feastdays of the Jews and of the Christians lies in the fact that these days were regarded not as days of penance, but as days of joy. For the Jews this attitude was commanded by God Himself, Who desired the Jews to "call the Sabbath delightful." [12] It is also indicated by the author of 1 Machabees who, in bemoaning the fate of the city of Jerusalem, says that "her festival days were turned into mourning, her sabbaths into reproach." [13] That the Jewish practices, like those of the Christians, reflected that spirit of joy can be deduced from the

[8] Sermo CCLXXX—Migne, *Patrologiae Cursus Completus (Series Latina,* 221 vols., Parisiis, 1844-1864), XXXIX, 2274. Hereafter cited as *MPL.*

[9] Canon 1—Mansi, *Sacrorum Conciliorum Nova et Antiquissima Collectio* (53 vols. in 59, Florentiae, Parisiis, Arnhem et Leipzig, 1901-1927), IX, 949-950. Hereafter cited as Mansi.

[10] Duchesne, *Christian Worship: Its origin and evolution* (translated from the 3. French ed., London, 1903), p. 46; McReavy, "Servile Work,"—*The Clergy Review,* IX (1935), 270.

[11] Exodus xxxi. 14; Numbers xv. 35.

[12] Isaias lviii. 13.

[13] I Machabees i. 41.

fact that the Jews never fasted on the Sabbath or on Feastdays, that they wore beautiful clothes, and celebrated the days with festive meals.[14]

(c) Jewish Observance Adopted, in Part

In the early days of the Catholic Church Jewish Christians continued to attend services in the synagogues. This they were free to do after the example of our Lord Himself and of the Apostles.[15] However, they also took part in the exclusively Christian meetings, which were held chiefly on Sundays,[16] and at which they could worship God in their own manner according to their belief in Jesus Christ. It was at these Christian meetings that the early Christians adopted part of the Jewish Sabbatical observance, because even though they were exclusively Christian, the services nevertheless followed the normal order of the Jewish synagogues. They were the Jewish synagogue services christianized both in form and in purpose.[17]

After the Church's break with Judaism the synagogues were abandoned by the Christians, but the synagogue liturgy continued providentially to serve its purpose in the new Church.[18] It contained no sacrifice, but provided a perfect setting for the new rite established by Christ. The new Christian liturgy was in fact merely a continuation of the Jewish liturgy of the synagogues.[19] In a word, the Christian Sunday, when substituted for the Sabbath in order to provide for a distinct form of perfect worship, assumed those of its obligations which were reconcilable with the law of the Gospel.[20]

[14] Judith viii. 6; Welte, "Sabbat," *Kirchenlexikon,* X, 1441; *Luke* xiv. 1; Esther ix. 17.

[15] Luke iv. 15-16; vi. 6; John xviii. 20; Acts xiii. 14.

[16] Acts xx. 7; 1 Corinthians xvi. 2.

[17] Fortescue, *The Mass: A Study of the Roman Liturgy* (London: Longmans, Green & Co., Ltd., 1926), p. 3.

[18] Joseph Husslein, *The Mass of the Apostles* (New York: P. J. Kenedy & Sons, 1929), p. 48.

[19] Duchesne, *Christian Worship,* p. 46.

[20] Villien, *A History of the Commandments of the Church* (St. Louis: B. Herder, 1915), p. 26.

Article II: Origin and Development of the Jewish Observance

(a) Origin in General

It is impossible to determine exactly the precise time when the Sabbath as a day of special observance came into existence. The first reference made to it in the Old Testament is in *Exodus* xvi. 22-30. This reference, however, points to it not as a new institution, but as one with which the Jews were already familiar. From this it may be deduced that the third commandment of the decalog only sanctioned legally an already existing custom of the Jewish people, or perhaps even only restated an already existing law, as *Exodus* xvi. 28: "How long will you refuse to keep my commandments, and my law?" seems to indicate.

It is certain that the observance of special days which were given over to rest from work and to devotion to prayer and worship was not peculiar to the Israelites. Traces, at least, of this have been found among heathen nations, such as the Babylonians and Assyrians, who distinguished the 7th, 14th, 21st and 28th days of the month from the other days, and set them aside as days of rest and sacrifice.[21] From this, however, it cannot be argued that the Jews borrowed the notion of the Sabbath from these or other nations. It is possible, though it cannot be proved, that this custom among widely separated nations can be traced back to primitive revelation. Friedrich Nötscher asserts: "According to the account of creation the seven-day period is a basic law for the ordering of the world, which even God Himself observed in the creation, in blessing and sanctifying the seventh day." [22] The most that can be said with certainly is that the Sabbath is the oldest of the legally prescribed feasts of the Jews,[23] that it existed certainly before its observance was promulgated as a law by Moses, and that therefore it is of very ancient origin.

[21] H. Schumacher, *A Handbook of Scripture Study* (2. ed., 3 vols., St. Louis: B. Herder, 1924-1926), I, 175.

[22] "Sabbath," *Lexikon für Theologie und Kirche,* IX (1937), 49-50.

[23] Welte, "Sabbat," *Kirchenlexikon,* X, 1438.

(b) Sabbath Observance

As indicated above, the Jewish observance of the Sabbath and Feastdays was twofold: abstention from labor, and devotion to prayer and worship. Since this study is restricted to the Christian precept of hearing Mass, it is concerned only with the latter element, namely, the sanctification of the Sabbath and Feastdays by prayer and worship.

At no time under the Old Dispensation was there any specific positive legislation commanding the Jews to devote the Sabbath to prayer and worship. There was, however, the command of God Himself that the Jews should *sanctify* the Sabbath,[24] and it was in accordance with this command, no doubt, that the custom arose among the Jews of meeting on the Sabbath for public prayer and worship. The temple, of course, was the great center of Jewish worship, and this was the scene of special observance on the Sabbath day. The usual offerings which characterized the daily morning and evening sacrifices[25] were doubled,[26] and the loaves of proposition were changed.[27] A sacred assembly of the people on the Sabbath for solemn worship was also prescribed,[28] but since the temple was not accessible to all the Jewish people, this prescription can hardly be interpreted as a general law binding all the Jews. It was precisely because of this inaccessibility of the temple that the Jews began to build synagogues and there held the Sabbath and Feastday services, which, as has been shown, foreshadowed and contributed so greatly to the Christian Sunday services. Outside of Jerusalem, where the temple was situated, the weekly meetings of the synagogue became the highest expression of the collective religious life of the Jews.[29]

Just when the synagogues had their origin is disputed. Some hold that they were of post-exilic origin, but there are good reasons

[24] Deuteronomy v. 12; Exodus xvi. 23; Jeremias xvii. 22.

[25] Numbers xxviii. 3-8.

[26] Numbers xxviii. 9-10.

[27] Leviticus xv. 5-8.

[28] Ezechiel xlvi. 3.

[29] Duchesne, *Christian Worship*, p. 46.

to believe that they were in existence in much more ancient times, that is, before the captivity of Babylon, under the Judges and Kings. It is probable that the scribes and priests sent by Josaphat to the people in the different cities of Judea [30] taught the people in their synagogues. From the various references made in the Old Testament to a renowned place of worship in Maspha [31] it has been deduced that the first synagogue was located there, and existed before the time of Jephte and Samuel.[32]

It was probably after the exile that synagogues became common, and at these the Jews gathered every Sabbath for services.[33] These services—christianized—later became part of the eucharistic Sunday services of the early Christians.[34]

(c) Feastday Observance

Besides the Sabbath, the Jews also celebrated certain Feastdays, some instituted by God, others instituted by the Jews themselves. On these days servile works were prohibited, and each festival had certain ceremonies and called for certain offerings peculiar to itself.[35] Those of divine institution numbered eight, namely, the Sabbath; Neomenia; the Pasch; Pentecost; the Feast of the Trumpets; the Feast of Expiation; the Feast of the Tabernacles; and the Feast of the Assembly or Congregation.[36] The feasts instituted by the Jews themselves numbered four: the Feast of Lots; the Feast of the Purification of the Temple; the Feast of the Day of the Given Fire; and the Feast in commemoration of the slaughter of Nicanor's army.[37]

[30] 2 Paralipomenon xvii. 9.

[31] Judges xi. 11; xx, 1; 1 Kings vii. 5; 1 Machabees iii. 46.

[32] Becanus, *Analogia Veteris ac Novi Testamenti, in qua primum status veteris, deinde consensus, proportio, et conspiratio illius cum novo explicatus* (Louvain, 1775), p. 217. To be quoted hereafter as *Analogia Veteris ac Novi Testamenti*.

[33] Acts xv. 21; xiii. 27.

[34] Fortescue, *The Mass*, p. 70.

[35] Becanus, *Analogia Veteris ac Novi Testamenti*, p. 285.

[36] Leviticus xxiii. 1-37; Numbers xxviii. 11.

[37] Esther ix. 17; 1 Machabees iv. 59; 2 Machabees i. 18; 1 Machabees vii. 49.

Of the Jewish feasts Christianity adopted the Pasch (Easter) and the Feast of Pentecost, which became the first Feastdays of the New Dispensation.[88]

[88] R. J. Sherry, *De Temporibus Sacris* (The Catholic University of America Canon Law Studies, Licentiate Dissertation [Typewritten Manuscript], Washington, D. C., 1923), p. 40.

CHAPTER II

ADOPTION OF THE SUNDAY

ARTICLE I. THE FACT OF THE ADOPTION OF THE SUNDAY

(a) Its Relation to the Sabbath

UNDER the Jewish religion the most important day of the week was the Sabbath. Christ Himself and the Apostles conformed to its religious observances,[1] and so it is not surprising to find that the early Jewish Christians continued to regard it as a day of special religious significance. As usual they frequented the Temple and attended the sabbatic meetings in the synagogues.[2]

From a very early period, however, they also adopted the Sunday.[3] In doing so they were prompted not by a motive of hostility to the Sabbath or to Jewish customs, but simply by a desire to have[4] for their exclusively Christian meetings a separate day on which they could adore unmolested the Messiah Whom the majority of their fellow Jews refused to recognize.[5] Consequently the Sunday was adopted not in opposition to the Sabbath, but side by side with it. There was no thought at first of substituting the Sunday for the Sabbath; its observance rather was at first merely supplemental to that of the Sabbath.[6]

In the course of time, however, as the break between the Church and the synagogue widened, the Sabbath became less and less im-

[1] Luke iv. 15-16; vi. 6; John xviii. 20; Acts xiii. 14.

[2] Acts iii. 1; Luke xxiv. 52-53; Villien, *A History of the Commandments of the Church*, p. 24.

[3] Acts xx. 7; 1 Corinthians xvi. 2; Apocalypse i. 10.

[4] Duchesne, *Christian Worship*, p. 247.

[5] Villien, *A History of the Commandments of the Church*, p. 25.

[6] Dumaine, "Dimanche," *Dictionnaire D'Archéologie Chrétienne et De Liturgie* (Paris), IV, part I, p. 892; Duchesne, *op. cit.*, p. 47.

portant, and eventually became entirely neglected. As a consequence the Sunday alone became the day reserved for the special weekly religious observances of the Christians, and it assumed those sabbatic obligations which were reconcilable with the law of the Gospel.[7]

St. Ignatius of Antioch (+ 107), in spurring the Magnesians to observe the Sunday, tells them they should conduct themselves "no longer observing the Sabbaths, but fashioning their lives after the Lord's Day, on which our life also arose through Him. . . ."[8]

Another important witness to the special observance of Sunday by the Christians is Pliny in his famous letter to Trajan (111-113), in which he says "they (the Christians) are accustomed to gather together on the stated day before dawn. . . ."[9] It is commonly held among authors that *stato die* refers beyond doubt to the Sunday. The value of this testimony lies in the fact that even a pagan mind was so impressed by the distinctive character of the *status dies* that he wrote about it to the emperor. Therefore the observance of the Sunday at that time must have been markedly in contrast to the other days of the week.

Dionysius of Corinth (175) in an epistle to the Romans writes to the effect that "today we have passed the Lord's holy day in which we have read your epistle . . ."[10] This testimony is of value for two reasons: it mentions the Sunday observance in a casual manner, very much in the same way as we would speak of it today, thereby indicating that it was an accepted tradition in the Church at that time; the reference to the reading of the letter, which was no doubt a public reading, suggests a gathering of the faithful on Sunday, at which the letter was read.

Tertullian (*circa* 200) exhorts the faithful to put aside worldly

[7] Villien, *op. cit.*, p. 26.

[8] Ignatius, *Epistola ad Magnesios*, 9, 1—Lightfoot, *The Apostolic Fathers* (London: 1898), p. 145.

[9] Kirch, *Enchiridion Fontium Historiae Ecclesiasticae Antiquae* (4. ed., Friburgi Brisgoviae: Herder, 1923), p. 23, n. 30.

[10] Eusebius, *Historia Ecclesiastica*, Lib. IV, cap. 23—Migne, *Patrologiae Cursus Completus (Series Graeca*, 161 vols., Parisiis, 1856-1866), XX, 390. Hereafter cited as *MPG*.

anxiety on Sunday and even to defer business lest they give place to the devil.[11]

Eusebius Pamphilus (+ 339), Bishop of Caesarea in Palestine, testifies that an entire treatise on the Lord's Day was written by Melito, Bishop of Sardis, in the year 170.[12] This indicates that the Sunday, meriting a special treatise, must have been a day of special significance, and its observance an established practice in the middle of the second century.

Civil legislation also bears witness to the fact that Sunday had become an established and recognized day of special religious observances among the Christians. The celebrated Edict of Constantine (321) is the outstanding example on this point. In this edict the Emperor ordains that all those living in the cities shall rest from all worldly business on the venerable Day of the Sun. Only those living in the country were exempt from this edict, and that because of the danger of the loss of the crops unless they were cared for even on Sundays.[13]

That this legislation was ordained with the view to a religious observance is attested by Eusebius Pamphilus who says that Constantine's chief desire was that he might by degrees make all men worshippers of God. That Constantine had the Christians especially in mind is evident also from Eusebius, who continues:

> To those who had embraced the divinely inspired faith, he allowed time and leisure for a free exercise of themselves according to the usage and order of God's Church, to the end that they might without any impediment be present at the performance of the prayers.[14]

[11] Tertullian, *De Oratione*, cap. 23—*MPL*, I, 1191.

[12] Eusebius, *Historia Ecclesiastica*, Lib. IV, cap. 26—*MPG*, XX, 391.

[13] Imp. Constantinus A. Helpidio: "Omnes iudices urbanaeque plebes et artium officia cunctarum venerabili die solis quiescant. Ruri tamen positi agrorum culturae libere licenterque inserviant quoniam frequenter evenit, ut non alio aptius die frumenta sulcis aut vineae scrobibus commendentur, ne occasione momenti pereat commoditas coelesti provisione concessa." — C. (3.12) 2.

[14] Eusebius *Vita Constantini*, Lib. IV, cap. 18—*MPG*, XX, 1166.

The Acts of the Martyrs also testify to the special religious observance of the Lord's Day. For example, in the Acts of Saints Saturninus and Dativus (304) it is recorded that the martyrs, in answer to the questions of their persecutors, professed that they never omitted to assemble with their brethren to observe the Sunday.[15] The Acts of these martyrs are undoubtedly genuine, and consequently offer a reliable testimony.[16]

From these testimonies it is evident that the Sunday was, from the earliest days of the Church, set aside as the chief religious day of the week for the Christians, and at a very early period prevailed over the Sabbath in this regard.

(b) Its Religious Significance

It may be mentioned also that from the earliest days of the Christian Church the Sunday was considered not as a day of penance or of sorrow, but as a day of joy. Barnabas in his epistle (96-98) testifies to this when he says: "We celebrate the eighth day in joy, on which Jesus rose from the dead." [17]

In further corroboration of this statement can be adduced the fact that from the earliest times Christians were forbidden to fast on Sundays, as is indicated by various testimonies.[18] On Sunday the Christians were forbidden also to pray kneeling, but were commanded rather to pray in a standing posture, which was an indication of the festive character of the Sunday.[19] St. Augustine, in one

[15] Ruinart, *Acta Martyrum* (Freiburg im Breisgau, 1802), Pars Secunda, pp. 378-396.

[16] Butler-Thurston, *The Lives of the Saints* (12 vols., New York: P. J. Kenedy & Sons, 1925-1936), II, 167, footnote.

[17] Lightfoot, *The Apostolic Fathers*, p. 261.

[18] Tertullianus, *De Corona Militis*, Par. 3—*MPL*, II, 79; *Canones Petri Alexandrini* (circa 303), c. 15—Mansi, I, 1283; Innocentius I (416), *Epistola Ad Decentium Episcopum Eugubinum*, cap. IV—Jaffe-Kaltenbrunner, *Regesta Pontificum Romanorum ad annum 1198*, p. 47, n. 311. Hereafter cited as JK. Council of Gangra (circa 340), c. 18—Mansi, II, 1108; Council of Saragossa (380), c. 2—Mansi, III, 634; *Canones Apostolorum* (c. 400), canon 65—Mansi, I, 43.

[19] Tertullian, *loc. cit.; Canones Petri Alexandrini, loc. cit.;* Council of Nicaea, canon 20—Mansi, II, 684.

of his letters to Januarius, explicitly mentions this when he writes:

> (Sundays) which are already celebrated after the Resurrection of the Lord, in a spirit not of labor but of quiet and of joy, because of which the fast is relaxed and we pray standing, which is a sign of the resurrection.[20]

Article II. The Manner of the Adoption of the Sunday

(a) Manner of the Adoption

It is difficult to determine precisely how and on whose authority the early Christians chose Sunday as the day to substitute for the Jewish Sabbath. It has been maintained by some that the adoption of Sunday was based on a formal decree issued by the Apostles themselves. Thus the Pseudo-Apostolic *Constitutiones Apostolorum* in Book VIII, chapter 33, assert: "Ego Petrus et ego Paulus constituimus, ut servi . . . dominico die vacent in ecclesia propter doctrinam religionis . . . ,"[21] and Caesarius, Bishop of Arles (503-542), makes the statement that the Apostles sanctioned that the Sunday be given over to religious solemnity.[22]

This opinion, however, supported as it is by no convincing proof, seems to be an unwarranted assumption. Certainly there is no evidence whatsoever pointing to such an apostolic decree either in the Sacred Scriptures or in early Christian writings. The silence of the Sacred Scriptures on this point would not in itself be conclusive evidence against the existence of such a decree. But when this silence is considered in the light of a corresponding silence on the part of all the early Christian writers, it does become highly significant. The early Christian writers, whenever possible, appealed to apostolic authority to support their doctrine. At the same time they took delight in showing forth the transitory observance of the Jews as types of the higher Christian observances which were not to pass away. And yet in the matter of the transfer of the Sabbath

[20] St. Augustinus, *Ep. LV* (ad Januarium)—*Corpus Scriptorum Ecclesiasticorum Latinorum* (Vindobonae, 1866—), XXXIV,[2] 202. Hereafter cited *CSEL.*

[21] Funk, *Didascalia et Constitutiones Apostolorum,* I, 539.

[22] *Sermo de Diversis,* CCLXXX, par. 2—*MPL,* XXXIX, 2274.

to Sunday they make no mention whatsoever of a substitution by formal apostolic decree.

As a matter of fact the Sunday, while it was sanctified in the early days of the Church in a distinctively Christian manner, nevertheless did not at first enjoy that completeness of sacred distinction from all other days which it universally enjoys among Christians today. It rather existed in the beginning on an equal basis with the Sabbath, which would hardly have been the case had the Apostles by a special decree formally prescribed its observance in the nature of a Christian substitution for the Jewish Sabbath.[23]

The history of the celebrated Paschal controversy offers a very strong argument against the establishment of the Sunday by formal apostolic decree. If the Lord's Day had been definitely stamped by the Apostles as the one great Christian festival, deriving its sacredness from the resurrection of our Lord, surely the Churches of Palestine and Asia would have hesitated to hold the annual celebration of the Feast of the Resurrection itself on any other day than Sunday. The fact that they did advocate its celebration on days other than Sunday indicates a less authoritative establishment of the Lord's Day as the great Christian weekly Feastday.

In view of these arguments the adoption of the Sunday seems rather to have been simply the natural result of circumstances and of the fitness of things. Quite probably, as Villien suggests, the adoption came about in this manner. The Jewish Christians gathered together for the afternoon service of the synagogue,[24] and after the meeting came apart from the other Jews to hold their own exclusively Christian gathering "in memory" of Christ. Since, in the beginning, not every Christian community had its own apostle or priest, many of the Jewish Christians had to travel a longer distance than was allowed on the Sabbath in order to assist at the Christian meeting. Of necessity, then, their journey had to be made in the evening after the Sabbath was over, and the Christian meet-

[23] Cf. Smith-Cheetham, *A Dictionary of Christian Antiquities* (2 vols., London, 1880), "Lord's Day," II, 1043.

[24] Cf. Schürer, *Geschichte des Jüdischen Volkes im Zeitalter Jesu Christi* (2. ed., 2 vols., Leipzig, 1890), II, 382.

ing consequently began in the evening and lasted till daybreak of the following day, which was Sunday.[25]

When the Christians eventually abandoned the Sabbath and its observances, they continued to sanctify the Sunday, and through a gradual development it became the foremost Christian liturgical day.[26]

(b) Reasons for the Adoption

Aside from the manner of its adoption, the important point for this study is that the Sunday, from the earliest days of the Church, has been regarded as the Christian day *par excellence.* Whether the first Christians did so intentionally or not, the fact is that they chose the day most fitted for the sacred distinction accorded to it. Various reasons have been adduced why the Sunday should be celebrated in a more solemn manner than any other day of the week. The chief of these is that the Sunday was the day on which Christ rose from the dead. For it was on the day of His Resurrection that Christ began to pour forth upon His Apostles and followers the grace which He merited by His death on the cross, and made manifest in Himself and in them the first fruits of the redemption. "The resurrection of the Lord," says St. Augustine (354-430), "has given us promise of the eternal day and has sanctified the day of the Lord." [27] This allusion to the Sunday as celebrated in commemoration of the resurrection is repeated constantly in Christian writings. For example, the Apostolic Constitutions ascribe this reason for the Sunday observance. [28] Pope Innocent I (402-417) says that the Apostles and followers of Christ, overjoyed on the day of the resurrection, wished that not only the day of the resurrection itself should be most festive, but that it should be celebrated every week.[29]

[25] Villien, *History of Commandments of the Church,* p. 25.

[26] Cf. Smith-Cheetham, *Christian Antiquities,* II, 1043. Cf. also St. Thomas, *Summa Theologica,* IIa, IIae, qu. 122, art. 4, ad 4.

[27] *Sermo CLXII,* caput II— *CSEL,* XXXIV,[2] 194.

[28] Liber VIII, cap. 33—Funk, *Didascalia et Constitutiones Apostolorum,* I, 539.

[29] Innocentius I, *Epistola ad Decentium Episcopum Eugubinum,* c. IV—*JK,* p. 47, n. 311.

Other reasons adduced are that the Sunday was the day on which the Holy Ghost descended upon the Apostles, and that the name "Sunday" reminded the later Christians of Christ as the "rising sun" of the faithful. In connection with the latter reason it is worth noting here that among the first Christians the first day of the week was seldom referred to as "Sunday," *i. e., dies solis*. This was because the sun was looked upon by the Romans as a god, and the name *dies solis* naturally came to be associated with pagan worship. The Christians therefore called the first day of the week "the day of the Lord"—*dominica dies*. Justin (c. 167), the first Christian writer to employ the term *dies solis,* used this term because he was writing for pagans, and even in using the term he qualified it by the words "ut dicitur"—"as it is called."[80]

When the Christians later began to refer to the Lord's Day as *dies solis* they supplanted the pagan connotation with the Christian one indicated above. Finally, it has been suggested that just as Sunday was the first day of creation, when darkness was removed and light appeared, so also it is the first day of the new spiritual creation, when the darkness of paganism gave way to the eternal light of Christ.[81]

[80] Justin *Apologia,* I, 67—Rauschen, *Florilegium Patristicum* (9 fasc., Bonn: Peter Hanstein, 1904-1913), II, 109.

[81] Council of Palestine under Victor I (c. 198)—Mansi, I, 712.

CHAPTER III

EARLY OBLIGATION OF SUNDAY ASSISTANCE AT MASS
(First to the Sixth Century)

Article I. The Practice Among the Early Christians of Attending Sunday Mass

It has been shown how the early Christians, from the first days of the Church, held their own exclusively Christian meetings on Sundays. Since the purpose of these meetings was to honor God by prayer and worship, it is to be expected that these meetings centered around the supreme act of worship—the Sacrifice of the Mass.

The Sacred Scriptures as well as other early writings bear witness to this fact. St. Luke relates: "And on the first day of the week, when we were assembled to break bread, Paul discoursed to them. . . ." [1] This text indicates that the very purpose of the assembly was "to break bread," or in other words, to offer the Holy Sacrifice. In Jerusalem it was the custom to celebrate the "breaking of the bread" every day, and therefore it was celebrated on Sunday, very probably during the Christian gathering.[2]

The *Didache* (80-100) testifies to the celebration of the Holy Eucharist at the Sunday meetings: "Die autem dominica congregati frangite panem et gratias agite postquam confessi eritis peccata vestra, ut mundum sit sacrificium vestrum." [3]

Another important witness to the attendance on the part of the early Christians at Sunday Mass is St. Justin (+ circa 167) who says:

[1] Acts xx. 7.

[2] Acts ii. 46.

[3] Funk, *Patres Apostolici* (2 vols., Tübingae, 1901), I, 32.

> Ac Solis, ut dicitur, die omnium sive urbes sive agros incolentium in eundem locum fit conventus. . . . Postea omnes simul consurgimus, et preces emittimus; atque ut jam diximus, ubi desiimus precari, panis affertur et vinum et aqua . . . et . . . distributio fit et communicatio unicuique praesentium, et absentibus per diaconos mittitur.[4]

The Constitutions of the Apostles (c. 400), in describing the ordination of a bishop, mention that the bishop-elect and the people, together with the priests and other bishops, all gather together on Sunday. After the ordination the Holy Sacrifice is offered.[5] In the light of the other testimonies relative to the Sunday gathering of the faithful for Mass, it seems not unwarranted to conclude that the people gathered not precisely for the ordination of the bishop, but rather that the ordination itself was assigned to Sunday because the presence of the faithful was already assured on that day.

St. Augustine, Bishop of Hippo, also bears witness to this universal practice of the Sunday Eucharistic service in a letter to Januarius. In bringing out the point that some observances among Christians vary with different localities, he mentions as an example that in some places no day passes without the offering of the Holy Sacrifice, in other places it is offered only on Saturday and Sunday, and in still other places it is offered only on Sunday.[6] From this it may be deduced that everywhere the eucharistic sacrifice was offered at least on Sundays, and naturally it took place at the usual Sunday gathering of the faithful.

Article II. The Obligation of the Early Christians to Attend Sunday Mass

(a) Lack of Positive Written Law

From these and other testimonies it cannot be reasonably doubted that from the first days of the Church there existed among the

[4] Justin, *Apologia,* I, 67—Rauschen, *Florilegium Patristicum,* II, 109.

[5] Funk, *Didascalia et Constitutiones Apostolorum,* I, 473-521.

[6] St. Augustinus, *Epistola XIV* (ad inquisitionem Januarii) — *CSEL* XXXIV², 159-160.

Christians the practice of attending Mass on Sundays. However, just when the first positive WRITTEN law imposing the obligation of this attendance appeared is disputed.

Many authors, among them Villien,[7] propose canon 21 of the Council of Elvira (306) as the first written legislation on this point.[8] Furthermore, to emphasize the enduring influence of this canon, Villien points out that Bishop Hosius, at the Council of Sardica almost a half century later (343), referred to it and used it as an argument against some other bishops.[9]

A study of canon 21 of the Council of Elvira, and also of canon 11 of the Council of Sardica (343) [10] which latter canon contains the above-mentioned reference of Bishop Hosius, leads to the conclusion that the enactment of the Council of Elvira was not directed specifically at Sunday Mass attendance, but rather at a broader obligation, namely, that of participating actively in the religious life of the church of that territory in which the particular Christian resided.

Certainly the words of canon 21 of the Council of Elvira are in themselves vague. Implicitly, it is true, they may refer to the obligation of attending Sunday Mass, but to interpret them as an explicit precept which imposed specifically that obligation is not warranted by the wording. When this canon is considered in the light of canon 11 of the Council of Sardica the conclusion that there is a direct reference to the obligation of attending Sunday Mass becomes even less justified. Bishop Hosius is protesting against those bishops who leave their own territory and linger in the territory of other bishops, intruding themselves into the affairs of a church which is not their own. In attempting to correct this abuse, he cites the aforementioned canon of the Council of Elvira, and makes the point that if lay persons are not supposed to remain away from their own church for a period more than three weeks, then surely it is not fitting

[7] *History of Commandments of the Church*, p. 28.

[8] Canon 21: "Si quis in civitate positus tres dominicas ad ecclesiam non accesserit, tanto tempore abstineat ut correptus esse videatur."—Mansi, II, 9.

[9] *Op. cit.*, p. 28.

[10] Mansi, III, 15.

or permissible for bishops to remain away from their own territories for a longer period. On the strength of this comment of Bishop Hosius, it can be safely concluded that canon 21 of the Council of Elvira was not specifically directed to imposing an obligation of Sunday Mass attendance, but rather to a more general obligation—that of taking active part in the spiritual life of one's own parish.

Consequently, so far as the prescription of this Spanish council was concerned, one could probably avoid the sanction imposed by it, by attending any meeting of his own particular church, even though that meeting were not specifically the Sunday celebration of Mass.[11]

Another fact which may be brought as an argument against the conclusion that the Council of Elvira legislated specifically on Sunday attendance at Mass is that, if this were true, it would be the only council of the first five centuries to do so, which would appear rather strange. It is true that Villien makes the statement that: "from the fourth century on the councils . . . had to multiply admonitions and prescriptions" in this regard. However, if he means by this that the councils multiplied prescriptions bearing directly on Sunday Mass attendance as an obligation, then this statement too is unfounded. He fails to cite any of these multiplied prescriptions, and an examination of conciliar legislation between the fourth and sixth centuries uncovers no prescription whatsoever bearing directly on this point. The most that can be discovered are various conciliar canons which are concerned with more general prescriptions.

Thus the First Ecumenical Council held at Nicaea (325) confined itself to prescribing the posture to be assumed while praying on Sunday.[12] The Synod of Syria (405) similarly ignored the question of attendance at Mass on the part of the faithful, and simply defined that it was fitting that on every Sunday sacrifice be offered.[13]

[11] Dumaine, "Dimanche," *Dictionnaire D'Archéologie Chrétienne et de Liturgie,* Vol. IV, part I, col. 965; Dublanchy, "Dimanche," *Dictionnaire de Théologie Catholique* (Paris, 1903), Vol. IV, part II, col. 1334.

[12] Canon 20—Mansi, II, 684.

[13] Canon 12—Mansi, III, 1170.

The Council of Laodicaea (between 343-381) contented itself with simply prescribing that the Sunday be observed in a Christian manner.[14]

In view of the questionable prescription of the Council of Elvira, which is really the only canon adduced as specifically imposing the obligation, and in view also of the lack of other conciliar prescriptions on this point during the first five centuries, it seems safe to conclude that until the sixth century there was no positive written law imposing an obligation upon the faithful to assist at Mass on Sunday.

(b) Existence of Obligation Arising from Custom

However, it must not be concluded from this that there existed no obligation, and that the faithful were free to attend or stay away from Sunday Mass as they saw fit. While there may have been no written law enforcing their attendance, there was in all probability an unwritten law, imposed by tradition and by the custom of the people, which the faithful could not neglect without somehow abandoning Christianity.[15]

That such an obligation, based on tradition and custom, must have existed may be deduced from various writings. Theophilus, Archbishop of Alexandria, in the late fourth century stated in an edict that "mos et decorum a nobis exigit ut omnem diem dominicum honoremus, eumque celebremus." [16] The *Didascalia,* in the first half of the third century, bears witness to the existence of this obligation, when it admonishes the faithful to put everything aside on Sunday and to gather in church, and asks what excuse he will offer to God who does not go to church on this day to hear the word of salvation and to be nourished by the Divine Food which endures forever.[17]

Similarly the Apostolic Constitutions offer testimony as to the

[14] Canon 24—Mansi, II, 569.

[15] Cf. Villien, *History of Commandments of Church,* p. 28.

[16] *Edict of Theophilus of Alexandria*—Mansi, III, 1254.

[17] Lib. II, cap. 59—Funk, *Didascalia et Constitutiones Apostolorum,* I, 171-172.

existence of this obligation. In one instance, in prescribing that the faithful gather together very diligently on Sunday in order to give praise to God, they enumerate the order of the services to be held, namely, the reading of the prophets, the preaching of the Gospel and the offering of sacrifice.[18] In another, in describing the order of the eucharistic service, they offer a prayer for those who are absent and who have a sufficient reason for their absence, thus indicating that the faithful were obliged to be present unless they had an excusing cause for staying away.[19]

[18] Liber VII, cap. 31—Funk, *Didascalia et Constitutiones Apostolorum,* I, 421.

[19] Liber VIII, cap. 12—Funk, *op. cit.,* I, 515.

CHAPTER IV

SUNDAY MASS OBLIGATION FROM SIXTH TO THIRTEENTH CENTURY

Article I. Positive Legislation Prescribing Attendance

With the beginning of the sixth century the first written conciliar law respecting obligatory Sunday Mass attendance made its appearance. The first council to legislate explicitly on this point was the Council of Agde (506) which stated:

> Missas die dominico a saecularibus totas teneri speciali ordinatione praecipimus: ita ut ante benedictionem sacerdotis egredi populus non praesumat. Qui si fecerint ab episcopo publice confundantur.[1]

(a) The First Written Law

With respect to this canon, which was the first explicit prescription on Sunday Mass itself, it may be asserted that even here Sunday Mass attendance itself was not prescribed, but rather taken for granted. However, in view of the fact that the canon commanded an entire Mass to be heard, it can certainly be said that it implicitly commanded the Mass attendance itself, so that thenceforth the obligation rested not only on custom and tradition, but also on written positive law. That the obligation was regarded as serious is evident from the fact that its neglect deserved a public reprimand of the bishop. The I Council of Orleans (511) repeated this legislation when it prescribed that when the faithful attended Mass they were not to leave until it was over.[2]

[1] Council of Agde (506), canon 47—Mansi, VIII, 332.

[2] I Council of Orleans (511) canon 26—*Monumenta Germaniae Historica, Legum Sectio III, Concilia,* 2 tomes and 1 supplement (ed. F. Maasen, A. Werminghoff, H. Bastgen, Hannoveriae et Lipsiae, 1883-1934), I, 8. Cited hereafter as *MGH*.

(b) Insistence Upon Hearing Entire Mass

A characteristic feature of the legislation at the beginning of this period was its repeated insistence on the obligation of hearing Mass in its entirety. This was necessitated by the practice, which had sprung up among the people, of leaving the church after the reading of the lessons.

St. Caesarius of Arles (+542), one of the bishops present at the Council of Agde, indicated this in one of his sermons, when he said:

> With a moment's reflection you will realize that Mass is celebrated not exactly at the time of the reading of the lessons, but when the offering and the consecration of the Body and the Blood of the Lord are made. You can read the books of the prophets, the writings of the Apostles, and even the Gospel at home, but the consecration you can only hear and see in the house of God. . . . Those of you who persist in their remissness will be condemned by the just judgment of God. Notify them, therefore, and tell them most explicitly that it is useless for them to listen to the readings if they leave before the end of Mass. (Writer's own translation).[3]

He also insisted, in another sermon, on the gravity of the obligation of remaining for the entire Mass, when, in reprimanding his people for leaving before Mass was over, he said:

> I do not grieve, beloved brethren, when you leave the church, because you inflict any bodily injury on me, but rather because I know that you, whom I desire to be perfect, sin so gravely against God.[4]

However, it is to be noted that St. Caesarius, while insisting on this obligation, nevertheless provided for those who had good reason for leaving the church before the end of the Mass. He mentioned specifically as excusing causes serious sickness and public necessity.[5]

[3] Caesarius of Arles, *Sermo CCLXXXI—MPL,* XXXIX, 2276-2277.

[4] Caesarius of Arles, *Sermo CCLXXXII—MPL,* XXXIX, 2279.

[5] Caesarius of Arles, *Sermo CCLXXXI—MPL,* XXXIX, 2278.

Finally, the same Saint, insistent as he was on the obligation of remaining for the entire Mass once the faithful were present, did not neglect to stress the obligation of coming to Mass on Sundays in the first place. He mentioned expressly that no one was to separate himself from the celebration of Mass on Sundays and remain at home idle while the others went to church.[6]

During the whole of the sixth century this insistence upon hearing the entire Sunday Mass appeared at intervals in conciliar legislation.[7]

(c) Legislation on Other Relative Matters

An indication, however, that this obligation of attending Sunday Mass was incumbent only upon those who lived near the church was given by the II Council of Mâcon (585) which, in prescribing Sunday observance, stated that if the faithful live near a church they were to go there and give themselves over to prayers and tears. Just why the Council prescribed tears as part of the observance is difficult to understand, since it is evident from many testimonies that the Sunday was to be regarded as a day of joy.[8]

Unfortunately, the insistence of the councils and especially of St. Caesarius of Arles on the obligation of the faithful to remain in church till the end of Mass led the lukewarm into the alternative of neglecting the beginning of Mass instead. As a result, the councils were obliged to focus their attention on the obligation to arrive in time for the sermon and instruction.[9]

Other councils reminded employers of their obligation either to bring those subject to them, such as farm-hands, swine-herds, shepherds and other workers of the field and forest to Mass, or at least to see to it that they had the opportunity of going.[10]

[6] Caesarius of Arles, *Sermo CCLXXX—MPL,* XXXIX, 2275, par. 3.

[7] III Council of Orleans (538), canon 29—*MGH, Legum Sect. III, Concilia,* I, 82; II Council of Mâcon (585), canon 4—*MGH, ibidem,* p. 166.

[8] II Council of Mâcon (585), canon 4—*MGH, ibidem,* p. 166.

[9] II Council of Clovesho (747), canon 14—Mansi, XII, 399; *Capitularies of Theodulph, Bishop of Orleans* (797), c. XLVI—Mansi, XIII, 1006.

[10] Council of Rouen (650), canon 14—Mansi, X, 1202; VI Council of Paris (829), Liber I, canon 50—*MGH, Legum Sect. III, Concilia,* II, pars II, 643.

As a practical measure to secure the attendance of all parishioners at Sunday Mass, the Council of Rouen (650) proposed that pastors appoint loyal and God-fearing men of each parish to urge the careless and negligent in this regard, and to report to the priests those who refused to comply.[11]

In general, it may be said of the seventh and eighth century legislation that only from time to time did it recall the general precept of hearing Mass, but it did concern itself more with the particular aspects of the obligation. This conclusion is based upon an investigation of the councils of that period. It is interesting to note that even civil legislation at this time prescribed the observance of Sunday by attendance at Mass. Charlemagne in one of his capitularies (789) mentions it expressly.[12]

The seventh and eighth century councils legislated but infrequently on the matter of Sunday Mass attendance. However, toward the end of the eighth century and at the beginning of the ninth the legislation once more began to insist repeatedly on this obligation.

The Bishop of Orleans (797) in a capitulary stated that "Sunday is to be so observed that besides the prayers and Mass and the preparation of meals nothing else is to be done." He further stated that if the faithful found it necessary to travel on Sunday, it was permissible so long as it was not done during the hours of Mass and prayers.[13]

The II Council of Chalon-sur-Saône (813) mentioned explicitly the remissness of the faithful with regard to the Sunday observance, stating that it was gravely neglected. It then continued: "Unde oportet ut authentica constitutione illius venerandae diei observatio juxta imperium domini imperatoris statuatur."[14]

[11] Council of Rouen (650), canon 15—Mansi, X, 1202.

[12] *Capitularies of Charlemagne*, cap. 80— *MGH, Legum Sect. II, Capitularia Regum Francorum* (2 tomes in 5 vols., ed. A. Boretius et V. Krause, Hannoverae, 1883-1897), I, 61.

[13] *Capitularies of Theodulph*, cap. XXIX—Mansi, XIII, 1000.

[14] Canon 1—*MGH, Legum Sect. III, Concilia*, II, pars I, 283. The council here no doubt referred to the capitulary of Charlemagne cited above.

In addition to these many other councils of the ninth century stressed this obligation.[15]

While the councils of the tenth century continued to insist on the matter of Sunday Mass attendance itself, they at the same time issued other prescriptions in order to facilitate compliance with this law and to eliminate matters which might be adduced as excuses for neglecting the Sunday Mass obligation.

Thus the Council of Tribur (895) prescribed that it was not lawful to cite the faithful before the courts on Sundays, and immediately stressed the obligation incumbent upon every Christian to attend Mass on that day.[16] The Council of Erfurt in Saxony (932) issued the same prescription, stating that it did so in order to make it easier for the faithful to attend church.[17]

Other councils of the tenth century confined themselves simply to stating the obligation of attending Mass, and to reminding the faithful that other pursuits should not conflict with the fulfillment of this obligation.[18]

All these points of legislation were made the subject of inquiry by the bishops on the occasion of their episcopal visitation, as is evidenced by the formularies contained in the *Libri duo de synodalibus causis et disciplinis ecclesiasticis* (c. 906) compiled by Regino of Prüm (+915), who wrote expressly for this purpose. The clergy and faithful gathered together in the presence of the bishop in what were called "synodal" or "parochial" gatherings, and the bishop made inquiries to determine the spiritual condition of the parish. Among the questions asked were: If on Sundays and feast-days all assembled for Mass? If anyone was so perverse and estranged from

[15] Cf. Council of Mainz (813), canon 37—*MGH, ibidem,* 270; VI Council of Paris (829), Liber I, canon 50—*MGH, Legum Sect. III, Concilia,* II, pars II, 643; II Council of Aix-la-Chapelle (836), canon 22—*MGH, Legum Sect. III, Concilia,* II, pars II, 710; Synod of Rome (853), canon 30—Mansi, XIV, 1007.

[16] Canon 25—*MGH, Legum Sect. II, Cap. Regum Franc.*, II, pars I, 233.

[17] Canon 2—Mansi, XVIIIa, 363.

[18] Cf. Council of Ingelheim (948), canon 6—Mansi, XVIIIa, 42; Council of Enham (end of 10th c.)—Mansi, XIX, 301; *Liber Legum Ecclesiasticarum* (994), canon 24—Mansi, XIX, 186.

God that he did not go to church at least on Sunday? If the swine-herds and other workers went to church and heard Mass on Sundays? If there were promoters in each parish, loyal and God-fearing men, who admonished the others to come to church and to assist at Mass? [19]

Article II. Enforcement of Precept by Sanction

The rest of this period is characterized by the Church's use of another means to enforce obedience to the precept of Sunday Mass attendance, namely, the infliction of penalties on those who refused to comply. It is true that this incentive had been used before,[20] but then it had been the exception. Now it became the rule.

Even the secular arm was enlisted to enforce this obligation by means of penal sanctions. Thus St. Stephen, King of Hungary (997-1038), issued a precept that all were to come to church on Sundays, except those who tended the fires. Those who neglected to come were to be punished.[21]

(a) Corporal Punishments

Sometimes these sanctions took the form of corporal punishment, as in the prescription of St. Stephen just cited, which ordered that the negligent Christian be handcuffed and have his head shaved. The Synod of Szabolcs (1092) ordered those who neglected to come to church on Sunday to be punished with stripes.[22] The Synod of Strigonia (Gran or Esztergam) (1114) ordered that those who neglected to observe the prescribed feasts were to be punished with a penance of forty days—or if their neglect was less culpable, with a penance of seven days.[23]

[19] Regino of Prüm, *Libri duo de synodalibus causis et disciplinis ecclesiasticis,* Liber II, cap. V, nn. 57, 63, 64, 68—*MPL,* CXXXII, 285.

[20] Council of Pavia (855)—Mansi, XV, 19.

[21] Collection of Ecclesiastical Constitutions in Hungary (1016), C. VII—Mansi, XIX, 371.

[22] Canon 11—Mansi, XX, 763.

[23] Cap. VIII—Mansi, XXI, 102.

(b) Fines

Later on these corporal punishments gave way to monetary fines. Thus the Synod of Pamiers in southern France (1212) inflicted a fine on property-owners who neglected Sunday Mass without a reasonable cause.[24] This prescription did not have its desired effect, which no doubt was due to the influence of the Albigenses who then dominated southern France. As a result, other councils renewed this prescription in rapid succession.[25] Finally, the Council of Albi (1254), which was held at the behest of King St. Louis and was attended by bishops from the provinces of Narbonne, Bourges and Bordeaux, inflicted a fine on those who neglected to attend Mass, or who left before Mass was over, but it excluded from this pecuniary sanction those who did not live in the city, or who were sick, or who had some other reasonable cause for absenting themselves.[26]

[24] Canon 7—Mansi, XXII, 857.

[25] Cf. Council near Toulouse (1220), canon 2—Mansi, XXII, 1135; Council of Toulouse (1229), canon 25—Mansi, XXIII, 200; Council of Beziers (1233), canon 5—Mansi, XXIII, 271.

[26] Canon 30—Mansi, XXIII, 840.

CHAPTER V

THIRTEENTH CENTURY TO THE PRESENT DAY

In the preceding chapter it has been shown how church legislation, adapting itself to the peculiar needs of the times, focused its attention upon the obligation of hearing Mass in its entirety on Sundays, and enforced the fulfillment of that obligation by the application of civil and ecclesiastical penalties. By the middle of the thirteenth century ecclesiastical discipline with regard to attendance at Sunday Mass had become well defined. The exact limits of the precept as it existed at that time were clearly determined. It prescribed attendance at Mass, the hearing of Mass in its entirety from the beginning to the priest's blessing, and—an element which has not as yet been indicated in this study—the discharge of this obligation in the parish church.

The period covering from the latter half of the thirteenth century down to the present day witnessed a repeated insistence on one aspect of the obligation, namely, that of attending Mass in the parish church. But it also witnessed the gradual relaxation of that obligation, and the final emergence of the precept into its present-day form.

Article I. Obligation to Fulfill Precept in Parish Church

The obligation of attending Mass in one's own parish church was at the beginning of this period of history by no means a new one. As early as the time of the Synod of Nantes, which presumably was held in the year 658 or 660, it had already become an explicitly defined precept, and it was renewed at intervals by the councils of the succeeding centuries.[1]

In order to insure the fulfillment of this precept, there was a

[1] Cf. cc. 1, 2—Mansi, XVIIIa, 166-167; *Capitularies of Theodulph, Bishop of Orleans* (797), c. 46—Mansi, XIII, 1006; Synod of Szabolcs (1092), canon 11—Mansi, XX, 763.

corresponding obligation on the part of the parish clergy not to induce or permit members of another parish to attend Sunday Mass in their church, unless they were on a journey or had permission from their pastor.[2]

(a) Observance Before the End of the Thirteenth Century

However, up till the middle of the thirteenth century there was no need of constant insistence upon these points by the Church, because for the greater part the faithful abided by this prescription as a matter of course. During the middle ages it was taken for granted that the Sunday observance should be centered in the parish church, because from the viewpoint of the faithful the parish was to their spiritual life what the signorial castle was to their temporal. It was there that they paid their duties to God, just as it was at the castle that they rendered homage to their feudal lord. Therefore the normal Christian would no more think of affiliating himself with a church other than that of his own parish, than he would think of rendering homage to a feudal lord other than his own. As a result, attendance at the parish Mass on Sundays was a precept well observed, and it was only rarely that it was necessary for the Church to legislate in this regard.[3]

(b) Struggle Between Seculars and Mendicants

So long as the fulfillment or neglect of the precept of attending the parish church for the hearing of the Sunday Mass involved only the rights of pastors, the situation was simple and difficulties in this regard were easily adjusted. In the course of the thirteenth century, however, a new situation arose. It became the source of great difficulty and controversy respecting the traditional rights of pastors over their flocks. This was occasioned by the rise of the Mendicant

[2] Synod of Nantes, cc. 1, 2—Mansi, XVIIIa, 166-167; *Capitulary of Rudolf, Archbishop of Bourges* (850), c. 15—Mansi, XIV, 951; *Precepts of Peter, Archbishop of Rouen* (1235)—Mansi, XXIII, 403.

[3] Cf. Villien, *History of the Commandments of the Church,* pp. 45-46; Franz, *Die Messe im deutschen Mittelalter* (Freiburg im Breisgau, 1902), p. 15; Gasquet, *Parish Life in Medieval England* (New York: Benziger Brothers, 1906), p. 21.

Orders—especially the Dominicans, Franciscans and Carmelites—and their building of churches and oratories in the vicinity of established secular parishes. It was not long before parishioners of the secular clergy began to fulfill their religious duties in the churches and oratories of the religious, with the result that the secular priests began to resent what they considered an unwarranted encroachment upon their parochial rights.

The motive behind this resentment was not only jealousy and hostility toward the Mendicants, but in many cases a genuine concern over the spiritual welfare of the faithful. Negligent Catholics when questioned as to the fulfillment of their Sunday obligation could very easily assert that they had discharged it in the church of the Mendicants, with the result that pastors were unable to keep their accustomed vigilance over the lives of the faithful. In addition to this, many Catholics manifested only too openly that they considered the monks to be more perfect and attended the religious oratories and churches out of contempt for their own secular pastors.

But the chief motive was an economic one. Many of the secular pastors depended for their support chiefly upon the offerings of the faithful at parochial services, and they saw in the growing custom of frequenting the Mendicants' churches a genuine threat to their own temporal well-being.

As a result, a heated struggle began between the parish clergy and the Mendicant Orders. The secular priests began to accuse the Mendicants of trying to draw the people to their own churches, and firmly insisted upon the obligation of the faithful to attend Sunday Mass in the parish church, an obligation which they rightly held was still in force. On the other hand the Mendicants, who had obtained from the Pope permission for the faithful to attend Mass in their churches and oratories, interpreted this concession in its broadest sense and deduced from it the conclusion that anyone who attended Sunday Mass there fulfilled his Sunday obligation.

(c) Conciliar Insistence on This Obligation

As might be expected, it was not long before this struggle began to be reflected in the legislation of the times. Thus the Council of Arles (1260) strictly prohibited the religious from receiving lay people into their churches and chapels on Sundays, and forbade them even to preach during the hours that Mass was being celebrated in the parish churches.[4]

The Council of Budapest (1279) was even more strict in this regard. It insisted that the faithful attend Mass in their own parish churches on Sundays, and asserted that they should not presume to go to the church of any religious order, even though that church were a parish church.[5] The same council, in order to insure the fulfillment of its prescription, inflicted severe penalties both upon the faithful who acted contrary to it, and upon the priests who received such members of the faithful into their churches. The former were deprived of the sacraments, and the latter were suspended from the exercise of their orders.[6]

During the course of the fourteenth century councils repeatedly returned to this point, asserted that its observance was badly neglected, insisted on the reverence due to the parish church, and punished remissness in this duty with severe sanctions.[7] The Council of Benevento (1378) was perhaps the strongest in its prescriptions. After reprimanding the faithful for condemning their parish church by going to other churches on Sundays for Mass, it commanded and prescribed and ordained that every priest was to ask before Mass if any parishioners of another parish were present. If there were, he was to eject them and refuse to start the service until they left. If they refused to leave he was to report them to the Bishop or his Vicar. Any priest neglecting this precept was to be severely punished.[8]

[4] Canon 15—Mansi, XXIII, 1010.

[5] Canon 33—Mansi, XXIV, 285.

[6] Canon 33—Mansi, XXIV, 286.

[7] Cf. Council of Trier (1310), canon 23—Mansi, XXV, 255; Council of Cologne (1310), canon 20—Mansi, XXV, 242; II Council of Ravenna (1311), Rubric IX—Mansi, XXV, 455; Council of Prague (1346)—Mansi, XXVI, 88; Provincial Synod of Dublin (1348), canon 4—Mansi, XXVI, 111; Council of Apt (1365), canon 12—Mansi, XXVI, 450; Council of Narbonne (1368), canon 84—Mansi, XXVI, 520.

[8] Council of Benevento, canon 68—Mansi, XXVI, 653.

In spite of these numerous prescriptions, the situation became increasingly worse. Apparently the faithful were not to be deterred from frequenting the churches of the Mendicants, even by the most stringent ecclesiastical precepts. The ill feeling grew apace between the diocesan clergy and the religious. Eventually it reached a point at which the parish priests, in order to break down the resented influence of the Mendicants, even went so far as to accuse them of spreading heresy.

Finally Pope Sixtus IV (1471-1484), grieved by the scandalous state of affairs existing between the secular and religious clergy, intervened in an attempt to effect a compromise and to establish peace. He urged the secular clergy on the one hand to look upon the Mendicants as co-workers in the vineyard of the Lord, to recognize the good work they were doing, and not to accuse them of heresy. On the other hand he forbade the Mendicant Friars to preach that parishioners were not bound to hear Mass on Sundays in their parish church, which they were obliged to do by law, unless they were excused by a reasonable cause. The Constitution "*Vices Illius*" (1478) in which he made these prescriptions was addressed specifically to the Bishops and clergy, and to the Dominicans, Franciscans and Carmelites of Germany.[9]

However, even papal intervention failed to establish peace. The faithful, evidently determined to throw off parochial as well as temporal feudalism, continued their custom of attending the churches of the religious even on Sundays. In the meantime the Mendicant Friars repeatedly applied to the Holy See for a privilege which would allow members of parishes to fulfill their Sunday obligation by hearing Mass in the churches of the religious.

(d) Relaxation in Favor of the Mendicants

Finally, Pope Leo X (1513-1521), no doubt recognizing the futility of trying to discourage a practice which the faithful were so intent upon following, issued a decree which stated that anyone who on Sundays assisted at Mass in the churches of the Mendicant Friars

[9] Sixtus IV: C. 2, *de treuga et pace,* I, 9, in Extravag. com.

satisfied his obligation and committed no sin, provided that his motive in attending was not one of contempt for his pastor.[10]

Article II. Total Relaxation of the Obligation to Attend Sunday Mass in the Parish Church

(a) Complete Relaxation by Force of Custom

This decree, opposed as it was to the entire previous discipline, but confirmed later by Pope St. Pius V (1566-1572), marked the end of the long and bitter struggle between the parish clergy and the Mendicants, and relaxed the long established precept of attending Mass on Sundays in the parish church.[11] This privilege was later extended on December 27, 1592, by Pope Clement VIII, who made it available with reference also to the churches of the Society of Jesus.[12] As a result of these privileges the obligation to assist at Sunday Mass in the parochial church no longer obtained, provided that Mass was heard in a church either of the Mendicants or of the Jesuits.

The difficulty, however, was not entirely solved, for there still remained the question whether the obligation could be fulfilled in other parish churches or in the churches of other religious organizations. In the course of time this problem also disappeared in view of the established custom of the people. It has been indicated that, even during the bitter conflict between the secular clergy and the Mendicant Friars, the faithful, on their own authority, were attending Mass in churches other than their own parish church. This usage grew, for the Sunday attendance at Mass outside of the parochial churches was not restricted to the privileged churches of the religious. Toward the close of the sixteenth century it had endured

[10] Leo X, litt. ap. *"Intelleximus,"* 13 nov. 1517—*Codicis Iuris Canonici Fontes*, n. 73. Hereafter cited as *Fontes*.

[11] Pius V, const. *"Etsi Mendicantium,"* 16 maii 1567—*Fontes*, n. 121. Cf. C. Paulus, *Welt- und Ordensklerus beim Ausgang des XIII. Jahrhunderts im Kampfe um die Pfarr-Rechte* (Essen-Ruhr, 1900).

[12] The decree embodying this privilege is not to be found in the *Fontes* or in the *Bullarium*. For its text cf. St. Alphonsus, *Theologia Moralis* (ed. Gaudé, 4 vols., 9. ed., Romae, 1905-1912), lib. III, n. 322.

long enough, and had become strong enough, in many places to effect the abrogation of the common law which had demanded attendance at the parish church.

St. Antoninus (1389-1459), Archbishop of Florence (1444-1459), testifies to this when he says that in the territories wherein exists the custom of hearing Mass in any place whatsoever, he who attends Mass outside of his own parish church does not sin. In those dioceses, however, where it is demanded that Mass be heard in the parish church, the law in this regard must be obeyed.[13]

It is significant that the Council of Trent (1545-1563) tempered the severity of previous councils and synods in this regard, and confined itself to recommending that the clergy admonish the faithful to go to the parish Church at least on Sundays and on the greater feasts.[14]

During the seventeenth century the custom of hearing Mass in other churches besides the parochial church became general, and finally abrogated entirely the common law in this regard. In support of this assertion the opinions of the moral theologians of the period can be adduced. Bonacina (c. 1585-1631) states that the precept of hearing Mass can be satisfied in any place whatsoever.[15] Gobat (1600-1679) teaches the same thing when he states that there is no obligation to attend the parish Mass on Sundays and feast-days.[16]

(b) Final Emergence of Ecclesiastical Discipline

As a matter of fact this custom of the people eventually effected that the precept could be fulfilled not only in other churches and public oratories but in any place whatsoever, as is indicated by the opinion of Bonacina cited above.

St. Alphonsus (1696-1787) in the eighteenth century also veri-

[13] St. Antoninus, *Summae Sacrae Theologiae, Iuris Pontificii et Caesarei* (4 vols., Venetiis, 1571), II, tit. 10, cap. X, p. 317.

[14] Conc. Trident., sess. XXII, *Decretum de observandis et evitandis in celebratione missae.*

[15] *Sacrae Theologiae Compendium Absolutissimum* (ed. De Laval, Londini, 1634), p. 503.

[16] *Experimentalis Theologia* (Monachii, 1669), Tr. V, cas. 5, p. 339.

fies this when he states it as the common opinion of authors that the precept can be filled in any place whatsoever, even outside of churches.[17]

This unrestricted freedom of the faithful to choose any place whatsoever in which to fulfill the precept of hearing Mass was apparently used by some even with regard to private oratories. This did not meet with the approval of the Holy See, which toward the end of the sixteenth century and during the seventeenth manifested its disapproval of this practice.

Thus the Sacred Congregation of Bishops and Regulars in 1594 stated that only those servants who are necessary for the service of the persons to whom the Indult of a private oratory had been granted were freed from the obligation of going to church to hear Mass on Feastdays of precept.[18]

While this response does not state expressly that other servants could not fulfill the precept by attending Mass in the private oratory, it certainly manifests the mind of the Holy See in this regard.

In 1686 the Sacred Congregation of the Council manifested the mind of the Holy See more unmistakably when it stated expressly that servants and externs who are expressly excepted, or who are not mentioned in the Indult, cannot fulfill the precept on Feastdays by hearing Mass in a private oratory.[19]

Apparently these and other similar responses of the Holy See were not considered by authors to have the force of universal law, for in the light of what has been indicated above, the common teaching even at the time of St. Alphonsus was that the precept could be fulfilled in any place whatsoever, even in private oratories.

Some authors took exception to this opinion on the score that private oratories could not be included. Thus St. Alphonsus, while admitting that the other opinion was certainly the common one, nevertheless recognized that the matter had become doubtful, both

[17] St. Alphonsus, *Theologia Moralis,* lib. III, n. 318; also Benedict XIV, *Opera Omnia* (ed. novissima, Prati, 1842), XI, *De Synodo Dioecesana,* lib. XI, cap. 14, n. 8.

[18] S. C. Ep. et Reg., *Pientina,* 15 mart. 1594, ad 4—*Fontes,* 1504.

[19] S. C. C., *Ampurien.,* 30 mart. 1686, ad 1—*Fontes,* n. 2889.

because of the opposition of respected authors, and also because of the wording which the Holy See used in granting indults regarding private oratories, and therefore adopted the opinion that externs could not fulfill the precept in a private oratory.[20] Pope Benedict XIV (1740-1758) was of the same opinion, holding that the precept could be fulfilled everywhere and in any church, except in a private oratory.[21]

The Holy See then adopted the practice of always including certain restrictions in the Indult through which it granted the privilege of the use of a private oratory. Among these restrictions there was contained the following: Mass could not be celebrated unless one of the principally privileged persons, namely, one of those to whom the Indult was granted and whose names appeared therein, was present. Another restriction was implied in the fact that the precept of hearing Mass could be fulfilled only by the privileged persons, and by those whose presence was necessary for the service of the priest or for the convenience of the privileged persons. Usually the Indult extended the right of thus fulfilling one's obligation regarding the Sunday Mass not only to the principally privileged persons, as explained above, but also to the simply privileged persons, that is, to their relatives (by consanguinity or affinity to the fourth degree inclusive) who lived with the principally privileged persons as members of the family. As a rule the Indult was extended also to the noble guests of the principally privileged persons.[22]

The Holy See, in excluding private oratories as places where the precept could be legitimately fulfilled by the faithful at large, made an exception with regard to the private oratories of bishops. As early as 1640 the Sacred Congregation of the Council stated in a response that all who attended Mass in the private oratory of a

[20] St. Alphonsus, *Theologia Moralis,* lib. III, n. 319.

[21] Benedict XIV, *De Synodo Dioecesana,* lib. XI, cap. 14, n. 10.

[22] Cf. Gattico, *De Oratoriis Domesticis* (Romae, 1746), c. 25; Feldhaus, *Oratories,* The Catholic University of America Canon Law Studies, n. 42 (Washington, D. C.: The Catholic University of America, 1927), p. 58; Benedict XIV, ep. encycl. *"Magno cum,"* 2 iun. 1751—*Fontes,* n. 413; S. R. C., decr. 23 ian. 1899—*Decr. Auth. S. R. C.,* n. 4007—*Fontes,* n. 6288.

bishop, whether the Mass was celebrated within his diocese, or outside of it, fulfilled the precept of hearing Mass.[23]

This special concession with regard to the private oratories of bishops was never abrogated. In fact, it was renewed on various occasions,[24] and was still enjoyed at the time of the adoption of the Code.

Apparently the Holy See made no further restrictions with regard to the place where the precept could be fulfilled, because authors of the nineteenth century still held the same opinion as that which had been held by St. Alphonsus, namely, that the precept could be fulfilled anywhere except in private oratories which were not those of Bishops.[25]

As far as the right of fulfilling the precept by hearing Mass which is said in a different rite than the one to which the person belongs is concerned, this seems never to have been denied. In response to certain questions asking whether it was necessary that the faithful hear Mass in their own proper rite in order to fulfill the precept, the Sacred Congregation for the Propagation of the Faith simply replied that the hearing of Mass sufficed.[26]

With these developments indicated, the Church discipline relative to the precept of hearing Mass has been traced to the status which it enjoyed at the time of the adoption of the Code. For the greater part it may be said to have been substantially the same as that which the Code has put into effect.

For the full consideration of the historical background of the precept of hearing Mass, there remains, then, only an investigation of the former discipline regarding Feastdays. This investigation will be taken up in the next and final chapter of the historical portion of this study.

[23] S. C. C., *Nullius,* 22 sept. 1640, ad 2—*Fontes,* n. 2621.

[24] S. R. C., decr. 22 aug. 1818—*Decr. Auth.,* n. 2585; 8 iun. 1896—n. 3906.

[25] Panzuti, *Theologia Moralis* (3. ed., 4 vols., Neapoli, 1840), I, n. 160; Craisson, *Manuale Totius Iuris Canonici* (ed. 6., 4 vols., Pictavii: Oudin Fratres, 1880), III, n. 4912; Konings, *Theologia Moralis* (Bostoniae, 1874), n. 406; Gasparri, *De Sanctissima Eucharistia* (2 vols., Parisiis, 1897), n. 963.

[26] S. C. de Prop. Fide (C. G.) 11 dec. 1838, ad 14—*Fontes,* n. 4778; instr. (ad Deleg. Ap. Aegypti), 30 apr. 1862, n. 10—*Fontes,* n. 4857.

CHAPTER VI

CHURCH DISCIPLINE REGARDING MASS ON FEASTDAYS

ARTICLE I. RISE AND DEVELOPMENT OF FEASTDAYS

IN the foregoing chapters the church legislation regarding attendance at Mass on Sundays has been traced from its beginning down to the present day. It now remains to investigate the corresponding discipline with regard to Feastdays. However, since from the sixth century onward, at least, the Mass obligation of Feastdays of precept developed precisely in the same manner as that of the Sunday,[1] it will not be necessary to trace the development of the law itself. The present chapter will be concerned rather with the rise and multiplication of Feastdays of precept in the Catholic Church, with the opposition they encountered on the part of the faithful when they became too numerous, and with their final reduction to the number now prescribed by the common law.

It was shown in Chapter I (p. 10) of this study that under the Old Dispensation the Jews celebrated certain Feastdays in addition to the Sabbath. The Apostles and the first Christians who had been converted from Judaism continued to observe these festivals just as they continued to observe the Sabbath. However, when the final break between Judaism and Christianity occurred the Christians retained only two, to which they attached an exclusively Christian significance. These feasts—the first feasts of the Catholic Church—were Easter and Pentecost.[2]

As a matter of fact, these two Feasts remained the only universal Christian feasts down to the third century, as may be deduced from the testimony of Tertullian (+222) and Origen (185-255). Tertullian is the first Christian writer who enumerates the Feasts celebrated in the early days of the Church, and he mentions only

[1] Cf. Villien, *History of the Commandments of the Church*, p. 124.

[2] Cf. Villien, *op. cit.*, p. 112.

Easter and Pentecost.[3] The testimony of Origen, which affords the same information, is of even more value, because in his controversy with Celsus it was necessary for him to enumerate by name all the festivals celebrated by the Christians.[4] Inasmuch as Tertullian and Origen are witnesses for the West and East respectively, it can be concluded that in the third century Feastdays in the Church had not as yet begun the rich development they were to reach in later centuries.[5]

Even after the abandonment of Jewish practices by the early Christians, Saturday continued to have a special religious significance in the Church. However, this veneration in the West was short-lived, for the Council of Elvira (c. 306) insisted that the faithful observe it as a day of fast, thereby indicating that it no longer enjoyed a festive character.[6]

In the East, however, the observance of Saturday as a Feastday was of much longer duration, for in the fourth century it still enjoyed a preeminence almost equal to that of the Sunday. Traces of this preeminence linger in the Churches of the East even at the present time.[7]

The fourth century witnessed the introduction of two other great Feasts—Christmas in the Western Church, and the Feast of the Epiphany in the Eastern. St. John Chrysostom (c. 354-407) testifies to the celebration of Christmas in the West before the close of the fourth century,[8] and it is certain that the Feast of the Epiphany was universally celebrated in the Eastern Church during the course of the same century, although it is impossible to determine the exact date of its adoption.[9] It is quite probable also that

[3] *De Baptismo*, cap. 19—*MPL*, I, 1222.

[4] *Contra Celsum*, 8, 22—*MPG*, XI, 1550.

[5] Cf. Kellner, *Heortology: A History of the Christian Festivals from their Origin to the Present Day* (trans. from 2. German ed., London: Kegan Paul, Trench, Trübner & Co., 1908), p. 17.

[6] Canon 26—Mansi, I, 10.

[7] Cf. *Constitutiones Apostolorum*, II, 59—Funk, *Didascalia et Constitutiones Apostolorum*, I, 171; VIII, 33—I, 539; Kellner, *Heortology*, p. 12.

[8] *Homily on the Nativity of Jesus Christ*—*MPG*, XLIX, 351.

[9] Duchesne, *Christian Worship*, p. 259.

the Feast of the Ascension took its rise during this century, as St. Augustine testifies to it in one of his letters.[10]

Since it is impractical for the purposes of this study to trace the origin of each individual feast, it will suffice to mention the Feasts observed at the end of the fourth century as enumerated by the first catalog of feasts contained in the so-called *Constitutions of the Apostles.* This catalog mentions Easter, Pentecost, the Ascension, Christmas, the Epiphany, the Feasts of the Apostles, the Feast of Stephen the first Martyr, and the Feasts of other holy martyrs.[11]

Since this study is concerned with the obligation of attending Mass, it will be necessary at this point to try to determine the precise nature of this obligation with regard to Feastdays as it existed in the first few centuries of the Church. Since early documents do not touch on the juridical nature of this precept, the status of this obligation must be deduced from the writings and practice of this period.

Unfortunately, an examination of these leads only to the conclusion that the obligation as existing in the first four centuries was not considered as uniformly binding, and that different Feasts were celebrated with varying degrees of solemnity. It is certain that on the more solemn Feasts, such as the Epiphany and the Feast of SS. Peter and Paul, the faithful gathered for the celebration of Mass just as they did on Sundays, as is evidenced by the sermons of St. Augustine, and by a letter of Pope Leo (445).[12]

From these testimonies, however, nothing can be deduced as to the existence of a real obligation to attend Mass on Feastdays during the first centuries. The most that can be said is that, as in the case of the Sunday, an obligation of attending Mass at least on the more solemn Feasts probably arose through the custom of the people. There was definitely no express legislation on the part of the Church in this regard.[13]

[10] *Epist. LIV* (Januario, c. 400), cap. 1—*MPL,* XXXIII, 200.

[11] *Constitutiones Apostolorum,* VIII, 33—Funk, *Didascalia et Constitutiones Apostolorum,* I, 539-541.

[12] St. Augustinus, *Sermo CCII—MPL,* XXXVIII, 1033; *Sermo CCXCVIII —ibid.,* 1365; Leo I, *ep.* XI, 2—Jaffé, *Regesta,* n. 60.

[13] Cf. Villien, *History of the Commandments of the Church,* pp. 117-121.

The sixth century offered the first written legislation pertaining to Feastday observance. The Council of Agde (506) enumerated certain of the more solemn feasts, namely Easter, Pentecost, Christmas and the Epiphany, and prescribed under penalty of excommunication that the faithful were to come to celebrate these feasts in the episcopal city. In order to enforce this precept it was forbidden on those days to celebrate Mass in the country chapels, and any priest who presumed to do so was excommunicated.[14]

This insistence upon the celebration of the more solemn feasts with the bishop found expression in many of the subsequent councils,[15] and it constituted the only point of difference between Feastday and Sunday discipline with regard to the hearing of Mass. From this period onward practically all legislation concerning the precept of attending Mass was applied expressly to Feastdays as well as to Sundays.

From the seventh century on the number of Feastdays gradually increased. The catalog of Feastdays contained in the Statutes of Sonnatius, Bishop of Rheims (600-c. 626), enumerated thirteen days to be observed as Holydays.[16] The Statutes attributed to St. Boniface in the eighth century enumerated sixteen.[17] While it is doubtful whether these statutes were actually issued by St. Boniface himself, it is nevertheless certain that they belong to his period.[18]

Article II. Power of Bishops and Its Curtailment

(a) Abuse Arising From Undue Multiplication of Feastdays

It is not to be concluded from these catalogs that the same number of Feasts was observed uniformly throughout the entire Church. Feastdays, both as to their number and nature, varied not only in

[14] Cc. 63 and 21—Mansi, VIII, 332 and 327.

[15] Cf. *e.g.*, I Council of Orleans (511), canon 25—*MGH, Legum Sect. III, Concilia,* I, 8; Council of Clermont in Auvergne (c. 535), canon 15—*MGH, Legum Sect. III, Conc.,* I, 69; IV Council of Orleans (541), canon 3—*MGH, Legum Sect. III, Conc.,* I, 88.

[16] Sonnatius, *Statuta,* canon 20—*MPL,* LXXX, 446.

[17] *Statuta S. Bonifacii, archiep. Mogunt. et Mart.,* canon 36—Mansi, XII, 386.

[18] Cf. Kellner, *Heortology,* p. 22.

different countries but even in the various dioceses. This diversity of observance is explained by the fact that from the very beginning bishops exercised the right of introducing new Feasts into their dioceses, and of excluding from their catalog Feastdays which they no longer wished to be observed. It is easily understood, then, that uniformity throughout the whole Church in the matter of Feastday observance was almost impossible. This explains, too, the tendency to multiply Feastdays which in the course of time resulted in an abuse that had to be corrected and remedied.[19]

It is not necessary for the purposes of this study to trace the progress of this abuse in the different countries. It will be sufficient to indicate the extremes to which it finally led. Thus in the twelfth century the Decree of Gratian enumerated forty-one Feasts to be observed, and among these are not included all the Feasts prescribed by particular bishops. The remaining Feasts of the year, the Decree continued, the faithful are not obliged to observe, but neither are they prohibited from observing them.[20]

The status of the discipline regarding Feastdays in the thirteenth century may be determined from the Decretals of Gregory IX (1234), which prescribed forty-five Feastdays in addition to the Sundays and particular Feasts of the various dioceses.[21] With this prescription Church discipline regarding Feastdays for the universal Church almost reached the highest point in its development, for in the following centuries only a few Feasts were added for general observance. However, local Feastdays continued to multiply, and in some dioceses reached a point where, in addition to Sundays, over one hundred days were prescribed for special religious observance.[22]

(b) Obligation of Attending Mass on Feastdays

It is important to determine here whether these Feasts, as enumerated in the *Corpus Iuris Canonici,* were Feastdays of precept as we understand them today, that is, feasts which carried an obligation

[19] Cf. Coronata, *De Locis et Temporibus Sacris* (Taurini: Marietti, 1922), p. 289; Kellner, *Heortology,* pp. 28-30.

[20] C. 1, D. III, *de cons.*

[21] C. 5, X, *de feriis,* II, 9.

[22] Cf. Kellner, *Heortology,* p. 25.

for the faithful to attend Mass. The decretals themselves make no explicit statement to that effect. They are rather concerned with imposing an obligation to abstain from work and proceedings in court, etc. Another decretal of Gregory IX obscures the issue by stating that Feastdays are to be observed according to the custom of each locality.[23]

Since it is impossible to determine the individual practice of each diocese, or in fact even of each country, due to lack of evidence on this point, the most than can be done is to try to arrive at some conclusion through indirect arguments. A Synod of Strigonia (1114) inflicted a penance of 40 days (or 7 days if the fault was less culpable) on those who neglected to observe the prescribed Feasts.[24] This indicates that Feastday observance was considered a serious obligation, and it is very unlikely that the obligation was restricted to the merely negative element of abstention from servile work.

Another argument which may be adduced is the following. When Pope Urban VIII in 1642 reduced the number of Feastdays for the universal Church, he forbade to be observed as Feastdays of precept any other Feasts which were held in veneration in particular dioceses, thus indicating that until then they had been observed as such.[25]

Finally, it is significant that when subsequent relaxations were effected in the Feastday discipline as established by Urban VIII, only the obligation of abstention from servile work was lifted. The obligation of attending Mass remained in force.[26] While these arguments lead to no absolutely certain conclusion, it may be deduced as very probable that Feastday observance did include the obligation of assisting at Mass.

(c) Correction of the Abuse by Pope Urban VIII

The excessive multiplication of Feastdays indicated above eventually gave rise to complaints on the part of the faithful. These com-

[23] C. 2, X, *de feriis,* II, 9.

[24] Canon 8—Mansi, XXI, 102.

[25] Urbanus VIII, const. "*Universa per orbem,*" 13 sept. 1642—*Fontes,* n. 226.

[26] Cf. Footnote n. 28.

plaints were based chiefly on economic reasons. The poor, especially, claimed that because of the over-frequent recurrence of days on which they were forbidden to work they were unable to obtain a sufficient livelihood. Other difficulties too manifested themselves. Many of the faithful took occasion on these days to indulge in laziness, or to engage too unreasonably in the pursuit of pleasure. Added to this, the intermixture of universal and local Feastdays gave rise to great uncertainty as to which days were of common and which were of particular precept.

Confronted with this disturbing state of affairs, Pope Urban VIII finally deemed it necessary to prescribe a uniform discipline for the entire Church in the matter of Feastdays, and to fix limits beyond which the local churches could not go. This he did on the 13th of September, 1642, in the important constitution *"Universa per orbem"* mentioned above.

In this Constitution Pope Urban enumerated the following days to be observed as Feastdays of precept in the universal Church: Christmas, Circumcision, Epiphany, Easter with the two days following, Ascension, Pentecost with the two days following, Holy Trinity, Solemnity of Corpus Christi, Finding of the Holy Cross; also the Feasts of the Purification, Annunciation, Assumption, Nativity of the Blessed Virgin, Dedication of St. Michael the Archangel, Nativity of St. John the Baptist, SS. Peter and Paul, St. Andrew, St. James, St. John, St. Thomas, SS. Philip and James, St. Bartholomew, St. Matthew, SS. Simon and Jude and St. Matthias; St. Stephen, the first Martyr, Holy Innocents, St. Lawrence Martyr, St. Sylvester, St. Joseph, St. Anne, All Saints; one of the more important patrons in each kingdom or province, and finally, one of the more important patrons in each city, town, or village, if such patrons were locally venerated. In addition Pope Urban decreed and declared that by the authority of his Constitution any other Feasts, whether universal or particular, and whether observed through precept, or custom or devotion, should thenceforth and forever not be observed as Feastdays of precept.

The importance of this Constitution of Pope Urban VIII lies not in the fact that it reduced the number of Feastdays, because it is evident from the above list, which enumerates thirty-five days to be observed under precept, that this reduction was negligible. Its importance lies rather in the fact that, besides creating a uniform discipline in the matter of Feastdays for the universal Church, it took measures to check the exercise of the power which local bishops enjoyed to prescribe Feastdays of precept for their own localities. For in the same Constitution Pope Urban admonished the bishops that, lest Feastdays, due to the importunity of the faithful, be once again too easily multiplied, they should for all future time studiously abstain from establishing new Feasts of precept in their dioceses, in order that universal uniformity might be maintained.

That this admonition of Urban VIII was tantamount to taking away entirely the power of bishops to establish Feastdays of precept in their dioceses other than those enumerated by the Constitution "*Universa per orbem*" is indicated by a response of the Sacred Congregation of Rites. To the question whether bishops could institute such Feastdays of precept, the Congregation replied in the negative.[27]

The catalog of Feastdays of precept as drawn up by Pope Urban did not long enjoy full observance. In the following centuries various Popes issued many particular indults to different localities relaxing the discipline which Urban had prescribed.[28] These indults, however, have no bearing on this particular study, for they relaxed the discipline only in so far as they lifted, on certain days, the prescribed abstention from servile work. The obligation to attend Mass on all the days enumerated by Urban VIII remained in force.

In some few instances, however, even the obligation of attending Mass was abolished, due to the particular circumstances of the time and place to which the indults were granted. Thus, after the French Revolution, when the Christian method of reckoning the calendar had been supplanted with a new method, and months were divided into decades instead of weeks, it became very difficult to observe the Feastdays as prescribed by Urban VIII. Accordingly, on April 9, 1802, an ordinance was issued by Pope Pius VII through the Cardinal Legate Caprara, which freed the faithful of France from the

[27] S. R. C., *Concordiae*, 23 iun. 1703, ad 2—*Decr. Auth.* S. R. C., n. 2113; *Fontes*, 5728.

[28] *Bull. Rom. (continuatio)*, cf. *Index Materiarum* under "festum," "missa," "festivitates in genere," "imminutio festorum," Vols. II to VII.

obligation of attending Mass on all days of precept except four, namely, Christmas, the Ascension, the Assumption and the Feast of All Saints.[29] The same Pope granted a reduction of Feastdays of precept to certain dioceses of Sicily, releasing them from the obligation of attending Mass.[30]

(d) Final Legislation Concerning Feastdays

It is impossible to trace all the fluctuations of Feastday observance as they appeared and developed in different localities. It is enough to say that in the course of time great discrepancies existed even in the same countries. The United States offers an example of this.[31] The Fathers of the II Plenary Council of Baltimore (1866) lamented the fact that there was no uniformity among the dioceses of the United States with regard to the number of Feastdays of precept. Some localities observed seven or eight; others observed only four. However, they allowed the discrepancies to continue, determining that the Feastdays of precept as they existed in the different provinces should be retained. The Patronal Feast of Our Lady of the Immaculate Conception alone they prescribed to be observed as a Feastday of precept in every province.[32] The prescription concerning the Feast of the Immaculate Conception was approved two years later by the Sacred Congregation of the Propagation of the Faith.[33]

The III Plenary Council of Baltimore (1884), wishing to establish uniformity among the various provinces and dioceses in the United States, saw fit to send a petition to the Holy See requesting that six days be retained throughout the country as days of precept, and that the rest be suppressed as far as the obligation to attend

[29] Pius VII, *Reductio festorum in dioecesibus Galliarum—Bull. Rom. Continuatio,* VII, 282.

[30] Pius VII, *"Paternae Charitati,"* 10 apr. 1818—*Bull. Rom.*, VIII, 1748.

[31] For a complete account of the status and fluctuation of Feastdays in the United States of America, cf. John Gilmary Shea, "The Church and Her Holydays," *The American Catholic Quarterly Review,* IX (1886), 462-475.

[32] *Concilii Plenarii Baltimorensis II Acta et Decreta* (ed. altera, Baltimorae, 1894), nn. 381, 383, pp. 198, 199.

[33] S. C. de Prop. Fide, decr. 24 ian. 1868—*Acta et Decreta* as above, p. lxxiv. Not in *Collectanea.*

Mass was concerned.[34] The six days selected to be retained were: the Immaculate Conception of the Blessed Virgin Mary; Christmas; the Circumcision; the Ascension; the Assumption and the Feast of All Saints. The petition was granted in a response from the Holy See the following year, so that uniformity was once more established throughout the entire United States.[35]

The final legislation on the subject of Feastdays of precept for the universal Church before the adoption of the new Code was contained in a *Motu Proprio* of Pope Pius X in 1911. In the Motu Proprio "*Supremi Disciplinae*" Pope Pius decreed that eight days and only eight days were thenceforth to be observed as Feastdays of precept in the universal Church. These days he enumerated as follows: the Feasts of the Nativity, Circumcision, Epiphany and Ascension of our Lord Jesus Christ, the Immaculate Conception and Assumption of the Blessed Virgin Mary, the Apostles Peter and Paul, and All Saints. No other Feastdays were to be observed as days of precept in any locality. If any of the Feasts he enumerated had been legitimately abolished or transferred, as, for example, was the case in the United States, no innovation was to be made without consulting the Holy See. And finally, if the bishops of any nation or region desired that any of the abrogated Feasts should continue to be observed, they were to refer this matter also to the Holy See.[36]

(e) Feastdays and Private Oratories

As a conclusion to this chapter it will be profitable to consider another aspect of Feastday observance which differs from that of the Sunday. It has been pointed out in the preceding chapter that the obligation of attending Sunday Mass could be fulfilled even in private oratories by the persons so privileged through indult. This privilege did not obtain on certain Feastdays, because it has been the

[34] *Acta et Decreta Concilii Plenarii Baltimorensis Tertii* (Baltimorae: John Murphy, 1886), n. 111, pp. 57-58.

[35] S. C. de Prop. Fide, resp. 31 dec. 1885—cf. *Acta et Decreta III Balt.*, pp. cv-cvii.

[36] Pius X, motu propr. "*Supremi Disciplinae,*" 2 iul. 1911, nn. I, III, IV—*AAS*, III (1911), 306.

constant discipline of the Church from the earliest centuries that on the more solemn Feasts Mass could not even be offered in private oratories. The Council of Agde (506), while it permitted Mass to be offered on other Feasts *"propter fatigationem familiae,"* forbade it on Christmas, Easter, Epiphany, the Ascension, Pentecost, and the Nativity of John the Baptist, and on other feasts which were considered very great. This is probably the earliest law on the subject.[37] Other early councils enacted similar laws, and prescribed that on Easter and Pentecost and all other particularly solemn Feastdays, all those living in villages had to celebrate the Feasts with the bishop in the city. This prescription was sanctioned by excommunication for those who neglected it.[38] The same discipline was in effect during the Middle Ages. In fact, the prescription of the Council of Agde, as given above, was simply repeated, and its neglect was punished by excommunication.[39] St. Alphonsus testifies to the existence of this discipline in the eighteenth century, enumerating the following feasts as among those on which Mass could not be said in private oratories: Easter, Pentecost, Christmas, Epiphany, Holy Thursday, Ascension, Annunciation, Assumption, SS. Peter and Paul and All Saints.[40] Finally, the same legislation is found during the period immediately preceding the adoption of the new Code. However, the discipline was modified to this extent, that of the Feastdays enumerated above, only those which were at the same time Feastdays of precept were included under the prohibition.[41] Thus it is evident that from the earliest centuries down to the adoption of the new Code the obligation of attending Mass on certain of the greater Feastdays could not be fulfilled in a private oratory, by reason of

[37] Canon 21—Mansi, VIII, 328.

[38] I Council of Orleans (511), canon 25—*MGH, Legum Sect. III, Conc.* I, 8; Council of Clermont in Auvergne (535), canon 15—*ibidem,* I, 69.

[39] C. 35, D. 1, *de cons.;* Council of Arles (1260), canon 15—Mansi, XXXIII, 1010; Council of Angers (1365), canon 33—Mansi, XXVI, 444.

[40] St. Alphonsus, *Homo Apostolicus,* (ed. nova, Taurini, 1890), tract. 6, n. 37; Cf. also Benedictus XIV, ep. encycl. *"Magno cum,"* 2 iun. 1751—*Fontes,* n. 413.

[41] S. R. C., decr. febr. 13, 1893, ad dub. XXIII—*Decr. Auth.* S. R. C., n. 3767; decr. 10 apr. 1896—*Decr. Auth.* S. R. C., n. 3896—*Fontes,* n. 6256.

the fact that the celebration of Mass was not permitted on those days. If, by reason of some special concession, however, the celebration of Mass was permitted, those privileged to satisfy their obligation could do so even on the Feastdays in question.

Part Two

Canonical Commentary

CHAPTER VII

BASIC LAW UNDERLYING PRECEPT OF SUNDAY OBSERVANCE

Basic and indispensable to the proper consideration of the precept of Sunday and Feastday observance is the determination of the question: Upon what law does the obligation of hearing Mass rest? Is it the natural, the divine positive, or merely ecclesiastical law? It is the purpose of this chapter to investigate this question.

The natural law prescribes that man in the course of his life should at times offer public external worship to God. This is the common teaching of theologians. For reason of itself manifests to man his utter dependence upon the Creator Who gave him being, and his consequent obligation of loving and honoring that Creator. Since man is composed of body and soul, and depends equally upon God for each, that honor which he is obliged to render must be external as well as internal. And finally, in view of the fact that man is a social being as well as an individual, and that society no less than the individual depends upon God for its existence, it follows that man should at times unite with his fellow men in offering public worship to God.[1]

[1] Suarez, *De Religione,* tr. II, lib. I, cap. I, nn. 12, 13; Herrmann, *Institutiones Theologiae Dogmaticae* (6. ed., 2 vols., Lugdini: Emmanuel Vitte, 1926), I, nn. 47, 48; Merkelbach, *Summa Theologiae Moralis* (3. ed., 3 vols., Parisiis: Desclée de Brouwer, 1936-1939), II, n. 685; Coronata, *De Locis et Temporibus Sacris,* n. 275; Vermeersch-Creusen, *Epitome Iuris Canonici* (3 vols., vols. I-II, 5. ed., vol. III, 4. ed., Mechlinae: H. Dessain, 1931-1934), II, n. 558; Prümmer, *Manuale Theologiae Moralis* (8. ed., 3 vols., Friburgi Brisgoviae: Herder & Co., 1935-1936), I, n. 327.

This prescription of the natural law as commonly acknowledged by authors is clearly indeterminate. It specifies neither the time nor the manner in which the prescribed worship must be rendered. Therefore the question arises: Does the divine positive law more specifically determine the obligation? Does it specify either a definite time or a definite manner in which the obligation must be fulfilled? Authors dispute this question.

It is certain that under the Old Dispensation divine positive law did further determine the natural law as to the time of its fulfillment, because it prescribed a particular day, namely, the Sabbath, for the discharge of the obligation. But with the advent of the New Dispensation, this prescription of the divine positive law, in so far as it designated the Sabbath, was totally abrogated.

(a) Various Opinions on Source of Obligation of Sunday Observance

Some few authors ventured the opinion that the obligation as engendered by the divine positive law with regard to the Sabbath was transferred, under the New Law, to the Sunday.[2] This opinion is very improbable and Sporer stands almost alone in its support. The very fact that the Apostles themselves continued for a time after the death of Christ to observe the Sabbath is proof in itself that Christ did not substitute the Sunday in its place.[3] In view, therefore, of the absence of arguments in its favor, this opinion may be dismissed as totally untenable.

A second opinion, and one that has drawn a number of modern theologians to its support, is that, while the divine positive law does not prescribe specifically the Sunday, it does prescribe that at least one day in the week be sanctified.[4] This opinion rests on the following line of argument. God Himself instituted the division of

[2] Sporer-Bierbaum, *Theologia Moralis Decalog.*, tr. III, n. 484—cited by Prümmer, *Manuale Theologiae Moralis*, II, n. 465.

[3] Prümmer, *Manuale Theologiae Moralis*, I, n. 465, c.

[4] Schmid, "Worin gründet die Pflicht der Sonntagsruhe?", *Theologisch-praktische Quartal-schrift*, LIII (1900), 12-26; Prümmer, *Manuale Theologiae Moralis*, II, n. 465.

time into weeks, and under the Old Law commanded that the seventh day, or the Sabbath, be given over to divine worship. The New Law abrogated the precept of divine positive law, but only in so far as it was ceremonial, that is, in so far as it determined the Sabbath as the day on which the prescribed worship had to be rendered. There is no proof that it abrogated the divine law precept in its entirety, and it would seem, therefore, that the obligation to sanctify at least one day of the week still binds. Consequently the obligation to observe the Sunday as incumbent now, rests on a twofold source—the divine positive law as manifested in the third precept of the decalog, which prescribes that one day be sanctified weekly, and the ecclesiastical law as manifested in the precept of the Church, which determines that day as Sunday.

This line of argument is not entirely convincing. Its chief weakness lies in the conclusion that the obligation to sanctify one day a week still binds because the abrogation of the precept in its entirety cannot be proved. It is equally true that the continuance of the obligation to sanctify at least one day a week under the New Law cannot be proved either. In view of this fact, and in view also of the fact that even the proponents of this opinion can only aver that the obligation "probably" endures[6] it seems safe to discard this opinion in practice. It is important, for our purposes, to note that this opinion states merely that the time for the rendering of the prescribed worship to God is determined by divine law. It states nothing with regard to the manner of rendering worship. Therefore, even if this view were definitely proved, it would not imply that the hearing of Mass on Sundays is obligatory by divine positive law.

(b) More Probable Opinion: Merely Ecclesiastical Law

The more probable opinion with regard to this question, and the common opinion of authors, is that proposed by St. Thomas Aquinas and Suarez. They maintain that the observance of the Sunday in substitution for the Sabbath derives solely and entirely from ecclesiastical law, and that the divine positive law prescribes neither a particular time nor a specific manner for fulfilling the natural law

[6] Prümmer, *Manuale Theologiae Moralis,* II, n. 466.

precept of at times rendering worship to God. Their argument is this. Under the Old Dispensation the third precept of the decalog was in part ceremonial, in so far as it specified a certain day for the special worship of God, and in part moral, in so far as it prescribed that man should depute some time of his life to worship. The New Law totally abrogated that precept under its ceremonial aspect, and it remained in force only under its moral aspect. Therefore, the precept of the decalog as it exists today prescribes no more than that man should devote some time of his life to the worship of God, determining neither a particular day for that duty, nor even that one day a week be devoted to its discharge.[6] This opinion has been adopted by the great majority of theologians, so much so that whereas St. Alphonsus designates it as *"communis,"* Vermeersch-Creusen and other moderns designate it as *"communissima."* [7]

It is this opinion, therefore, which will be adopted by the writer, and it will be applied to those particular problems arising in the course of this study upon which it may have a bearing. To sum up: The natural law prescribes that man at times in the course of his life should devote himself to the external public cult of God.

The divine positive law, as contained in the third precept of the decalog, and as effective under the New Dispensation, confirms this prescription of the natural law, without further determining it.

The ecclesiastical law, as contained in the precept of the Church, more accurately determines the natural and divine positive law by assigning a particular day—the Sunday, and a specific manner—the hearing of Mass—for the discharge of the prescribed cult.

It is evident that the ecclesiastical law is most conformable to the natural and divine positive law, in so far as it is morally necessary that those laws be more specifically determined, lest society,

[6] St. Thomas Aquinas, *Summa Theologica,* IIa IIae, q. 122, art. 4, cap. 1, nn. 1-7; Suarez *De Religione,* tr. II, lib. I, cap. 1, n. 16.

[7] St. Alphonsus, *Theologia Moralis,* lib. III, nn. 263, 265; Vermeersch-Creusen, *Epitome,* II, n. 558; Noldin-Schmitt, *De Praeceptis Dei et Ecclesiae,* (25. ed., Oeniponte/Lipsiae: Felicianus Rauch, 1938), n. 256; Coronata, *De Locis et Temporibus Sacris,* n. 275; Wernz, *Ius Decretalium,* III, n. 396; Iorio, *Theologia Moralis* (6. ed., 3 vols., Neapoli (Italia): M. D'Auria, 1938-1939), II, n. 123; Merkelbach, *Summa Theologiae Moralis,* II, n. 685.

lacking a public and authoritative designation of a determined time for public worship, would scarcely ever gather for this purpose, and also in so far as it closely parallels the divine positive law as effective under the Old Dispensation, setting aside one day a week in addition to other special Feastdays for the discharge of this obligation.[8]

It must be kept in mind, however, that the Church was under no strict obligation to select the Sunday, or even to depute one day a week for the special worship of God. Even now it is within her absolute power to change this precept, but since it has been canonized by so many centuries of faithful observance and has assumed such great spiritual significance, a sufficient cause could scarcely arise to warrant such a drastic procedure.[9]

(c) Obligation of Hearing Mass

From the opinion of St. Thomas and Suarez adopted above, it follows that the obligation of hearing Mass on Sundays and Feastdays cannot be attributed to any prescription of the divine positive law. For if the designation of the Sunday as the day on which special worship must be given to God arises solely from ecclesiastical law, then the obligation of hearing Mass on that day arises from the same source. In fact, it cannot be proved that there is an obligation based on divine positive law of hearing Mass even sometimes during the year or during one's lifetime. Suarez explains that Christ Himself gave to the Church a divine precept of offering sacrifice, but left entirely to the Church itself the determination of the time and frequency of the offering.[10] Granting that a divine precept commands the offering of sacrifice, it cannot be deduced that there is an obligation arising from divine law on the part of the faithful to assist at the sacrifice. Suarez himself admits this. Therefore, the most that can be said is that the hearing of Mass is most conformable to the divine law, and that it is eminently fitting and proper

[8] Coronata, *De Locis et Temporibus Sacris,* n. 288.

[9] Wernz, *Ius Decretalium,* III, n. 396; Coronata, *De Locis et Temporibus Sacris,* n. 275; Noldin-Schmitt, *De Praeceptis,* n. 256, c.

[10] Suarez, *De Religione,* tr. II, lib. I, cap. III, nn. 9, 10.

that the faithful should at times perform this act of supreme worship. Ecclesiastical law has determined the obligation of the faithful in this regard by imposing the precept of hearing Mass on Sundays and Feastdays.[11]

If it be objected that the natural law, confirmed by the divine positive law, obliges the faithful to hear Mass at least sometimes during the course of life in so far as it prescribes that man should devote himself to public external worship, it may be answered that, while the Sacrifice of the Mass is indeed the most sublime form of public external worship, it is nevertheless not the only form, and man could discharge his natural law obligation in some other way.

Therefore, as the conclusion of this chapter, it may be stated once again that the precept of hearing Mass on Sundays and Feastdays, and in fact at any time at all, arises solely from ecclesiastical law, and not from the natural or the divine positive law.

[11] Gasparri, *Tractatus Canonicus de Sanctissima Eucharistia* (2 vols. Parisiis: Delhomme et Briguet, 1897), n. 947; Coronata, *De Locis et Temporibus Sacris*, n. 291.

CHAPTER VIII

CODE LEGISLATION PERTAINING EXCLUSIVELY TO FEASTDAYS

THE precept of hearing Mass on Feastdays, and the obligations flowing from it, are identical in almost every respect with the precept and attendant obligations of hearing Mass on Sundays. Since certain prescriptions of law, however, pertain specifically to Feastdays, such as those regulating the institution, transfer and abolition, it will be the purpose of this chapter to consider these prescriptions in order. Once this has been accomplished, the conclusions drawn in the chapters that follow will apply equally to the Sunday and the Feastday precept.

The term "Feastday" as used throughout this study will denote exclusively those days on which, by precept of the competent ecclesiastical authority, the faithful are obliged to abstain from servile work and assist at the Holy Sacrifice of the Mass. Therefore, it will never include those feasts of mere devotion, on which the faithful are not obliged to hear Mass.

The present chapter will consider, first, Feastdays of universal law, and then Feastdays of particular law.

ARTICLE I. INSTITUTION, TRANSFER AND ABOLITION OF FEASTDAYS OF UNIVERSAL LAW

Canon 1244, § 1: Dies festos itemque dies abstinentiae et ieiunii, universae Ecclesiae communes, constituere, transferre, abolere, unius est supremae ecclesiasticae auctoritatis.

§ 2: Ordinarii locorum peculiares suis dioecesibus seu locis dies festos aut dies abstinentiae et ieiunii possunt, per modum tantum actus, indicere.

(a) Exclusive Right of Church to Legislate on Religious Feastdays

Paragraph one of canon 1244 reserves the power to establish, transfer or abolish Feastdays common to the universal Church exclusively to the supreme ecclesiastical authority.

The Church has an exclusive right to legislate for the faithful with regard to Feastdays. This right is based on the power given it by Christ to regulate all matters pertaining to the practice of sacred worship and the administration of spiritual things. And it is evident that the observance of Feastdays is related most closely to the practice of divine worship and to the nurturing of the spiritual life of the faithful. Hence it follows that the civil authority lacks all power over religious Feastdays, and can neither institute, nor transfer, nor abolish them. That power belongs solely and exclusively to the Church. However, there is nothing to prevent the state from prohibiting those abuses which, insofar as their prevention falls under its authority, are incompatible with the proper observance of legitimately established Feastdays. In fact, its interest and cooperation in this regard are to be encouraged as beneficial to the Church.[1]

The inherent power of the Church relative to Feastdays has been exercised from the earliest days of her existence. It has manifested itself at times through the medium of custom, and at other times, through the medium of written law, both universal and particular. Canon 1244 regulates the present discipline with regard to the institution, transfer and abolition of Feastdays.

(b) Supreme Ecclesiastical Authority

By the supreme ecclesiastical authority, which, according to paragraph one of canon 1244, can alone institute, transfer or abolish Feastdays common to the universal Church, is meant the Pope or an ecumenical council. Some authors restrict the meaning of the term

[1] Van Hove, *De Legibus Ecclesiasticis* (Mechlinae: H. Dessain, 1930), n. 131; DeMeester, *Iuris Canonici et Iuris Canonico-civilis Compendium* (editio nova, 3 vols. in 4, Brugis: Desclée, De Brouwer et Si, 1921-1928), n. 1240; Cocchi, *Commentarium in Codicem Iuris Canonici* (5 vols. in 8, Taurini-Romae: Marietti, 1922-1930), III, n. 75; Wernz, *Ius Decretalium*, III, n. 397.

"*suprema ecclesiastica auctoritas*" to the Pope, claiming that he alone can exercise universal jurisdiction over the Church.[2] However, there can be little doubt that an ecumenical council is competent in this regard, since it has power to legislate for the universal Church.[3]

The Sacred Roman Congregations are not of their very nature included under the term "*suprema ecclesiastica auctoritas*," since they lack the true and absolute power of legislating for the universal Church. Hence, any prescription they might make relative to the institution, transfer or abolition of Feastdays common to the universal Church would have the force of universal law only if it were antecedently or subsequently approved or confirmed by the Pope in a special manner.[4]

(c) Notion of Institution, Transfer and Abolition

The institution of a Feastday may be defined as the designation of some particular day as one to which there is attached the obligation of hearing Mass and abstaining from servile work. The abolition of a Feastday may be defined as the withdrawal of that obligation from some particular day to which it has already been attached. And the transfer of a Feastday may be defined as the assigning of the celebration of a Feast to a day other than that on which it is usually celebrated, in such a way that not only the Office and Mass of the Feast are transferred, but also the obligation of hearing Mass and of abstaining from servile work.[5]

Canon 1244, § 1, states explicitly that only the Pope or an Ecumenical Council can constitute, transfer or abolish Feastdays that are common to the universal Church. That this exclusive competence is not limited to such feasts, however, may be deduced from the second paragraph of the same canon. For the sake of clarity it will be profitable to enumerate here all those other powers which

[2] Cocchi, *Commentarium*, III, n. 75; Iorio, *Theologia Moralis*, II, n. 123.

[3] Canon 228, § 1; Coronata, *De Locis et Temporibus Sacris*, n. 274; De Meester, *Compendium*, n. 1240; Vermeersch-Creusen, *Epitome*, II, n. 552.

[4] Wernz, *Ius Decretalium*, I, n. 92; Coronata, *De Locis et Temporibus Sacris*, n. 274.

[5] Canon 339, § 3.

are reserved exclusively to the supreme ecclesiastical authority. The local ordinary can designate a Feastday for his own diocese or territory, but only by way of act. This is the only power which is conceded him by the Code. Therefore, only the Pope or an ecumenical council can:

1. Constitute permanent Feastdays in any diocese or territory.

2. Transfer either permanently or temporarily Feastdays which already exist in any diocese or territory.

3. Abolish permanently or for a time Feastdays which already exist in any diocese or territory.

The reasons underlying these conclusions will be indicated in Article III of this chapter, which will offer a closer study of canon 1244, § 2.

Article II. Present Status of Feastdays of Universal Law

Canon 1247, § 1: Dies festi sub praecepto in universa Ecclesia sunt tantum: Omnes et singuli dies dominici, festa Nativitatis, Circumcisionis, Epiphaniae, Ascensionis et sanctissimi Corporis Christi, Immaculatae Conceptionis et Assumptionis Almae Genitricis Dei Mariae, sancti Ioseph eius sponsi, Beatorum Petri et Pauli Apostolorum, Omnium denique Sanctorum.

§ 2: Ecclesiastico praecepto dies festi Patronorum non subiacent; locorum autem Ordinarii possunt sollemnitatem exteriorem transferre ad dominicam proxime sequentem.

§ 3: Sicubi aliquod festum ex enumeratis legitime sit abolitum vel translatum, nihil inconsulta Sede Apostolica innovetur.

(a) Catalog as Enumerated in Code

The catalog of Feastdays drawn up in paragraph 1 of this canon corresponds almost exactly to that of Pius X, as incorporated in his *Motu Proprio "Supremi Disciplinae"* of July 2, 1911. It differs only in that it includes the Feasts of St. Joseph and of Corpus Christi, which were not contained in the *Motu Proprio.*[6]

By virtue of this paragraph, all other Feastdays, whether of common or particular law, were abrogated. Therefore the obligation of hearing Mass on feasts other than those enumerated in canon 1247, § 1, whether it bound the entire Church or some diocese or territory, or whether it existed by virtue of a particular law, or in view of a local custom even a hundred years old, or even by special grant of the Holy See, ceased. This is clearly stated in a response of the Pontifical Commission for the authentic Interpretation of the Code given on February 17, 1918, which asserted that on such days the faithful were no longer obliged to hear Mass.[7] Therefore it may be asserted with certainty that today the only Feasts other than those enumerated in canon 1247, § 1, which can possibly be of precept are those which have been granted to some particular territory by a special concession of the Holy See since the adoption of the Code, or which have been prescribed by the local ordinary *"per modum actus"* in accordance with the power granted him by canon 1244, § 2.

There seems to be no valid reason why in the future a Feastday may not be introduced by legitimate custom, since the Code does not reprobate the establishment of a custom in this regard. Since, however, it would be necessary that the community have the intention of binding itself by the obligation of hearing Mass in order that such a custom could attain the force of law [8] it seems hardly likely that any such Feastday will ever eventuate.

Canon 1247, § 2, declares first of all that patronal Feasts are not days of precept, and then concedes to local ordinaries the power of transferring the external solemnity of these Feasts to the Sunday immediately following.

This paragraph, in declaring that the Feasts of Patrons are not of precept, does not modify the prescription of paragraph one. It

[6] Pius X, motu proprio *"Supremi Disciplinae,"* 2 iul. 1911, n. I—*AAS,* III (1911), 305.

[7] P. C. I., resp. 17 feb. 1918—*AAS,* X (1918), 170. Cf. also Bouscaren, *The Canon Law Digest* (2 vols. and supplement, Milwaukee: Bruce, 1934-1937-1941), I, 585. Cited hereafter as *CLD.*

[8] Canon 28.

merely declares that Patronal Feasts, as such, do not carry the obligation of hearing Mass. If the Patronal Feast of any given locality is at the same time one of the Feastdays enumerated in the first paragraph of canon 1247, then, by reason of that very fact, it is a day of precept. For example, the Feast of the Immaculate Conception, even though it is the Patronal Feast of the United States, is nevertheless a Feastday of precept in this country. Therefore, the declaration of canon 1247, § 2, is no more than the application of the abrogative effects of paragraph one to a particular kind of Feastday, as indicated above. Paragraph two, no less than paragraph one, is also taken over bodily from the *Motu Proprio Supremi Disciplinae* of Pius X,[9] and the Pontiff's reason for expressly excluding Patronal Feasts as days of precept was no doubt to preclude any speculation on the matter, because before his time it had been customary to observe as days of precept not only the Patronal Feast of each kingdom or province, but even that of each town or city or village.[10]

The second part of canon 1247, § 2, which grants to local ordinaries the power to transfer the external solemnity of Patronal Feasts to the following Sunday is beyond the scope of this study, and therefore merits no distinct consideration. It may be pointed out, however, that if the Local Ordinary transfers the external solemnity of a Patronal Feast which is at the same time enumerated in the catalog of paragraph one, the obligation to hear Mass is not thereby transferred but remains attached to the Feastday itself. This is clear not only from canon 1247, § 2, which gives him the power to transfer the external solemnity and nothing more, but also from canon 1244, § 2, which, while it grants him the power to designate Feastdays for his territory *"per modum actus,"* grants him no power to transfer Feastdays prescribed by the common law of the Church, for this is reserved to the supreme ecclesiastical authority.[11] Therefore, if a local ordinary attempted to transfer the obligation of hearing Mass from such a Patronal Feastday to the succeeding Sunday,

9 Under n. III—*AAS,* III (1910), 306.

10 Cf. Urban VIII, const. *"Universa per orbem,"* 13 sept. 1642—*Fontes,* n. 226.

11 Canon 1244, § 1.

and thereby attempted to remove the obligation from the day itself, he would exceed the limits of his power as granted by either of these canons.

(b) Feastdays in Effect in the United States

Canon 1247, § 3, modifies the prescription of canon 1247, § 1, by prescribing that, if any of the Feastdays enumerated therein have been legitimately abolished in any place, then no innovation is to be made without consulting the Holy See.

This, in effect, reduced the number of Feastdays prescribed by paragraph one, relative to those places where, prior to the adoption of the Code, such a legitimate abolition had been effected. By legitimate abolition is meant in general the abolition by some special provision of law, whether it be by concordat, by indult or even by legitimate custom.[12] Therefore, in all those places where a Feastday had been abolished in any one of these ways, that Feastday is not of obligation in the present even though it be included in the catalog of canon 1247, § 1, unless the Holy See itself has determined otherwise.

Many territories throughout the world have been affected by this prescription of paragraph three, inasmuch as prior to the Code they had secured such a legitimate abolition of one or the other Feastday. The present study, however, will confine itself to a special consideration of this paragraph as affecting the United States of America.

It has been pointed out in the historical portion of this work that for a long time there was no uniformity in the matter of Feastdays in the States and Territories of America. The Second Plenary Council of Baltimore (1866), while lamenting the fact that no uniformity existed, took no measures to effect the desired uniformity. The Third Plenary Council (1884), however, sent a petition to the Holy See requesting that six days be retained as Feastdays and that all other days observed throughout the States and Territories be suppressed as days of precept.

The six days selected to be retained were the following: The Immaculate Conception of the Blessed Virgin Mary; Christmas; the Circumcision; the Ascension; the Assumption of the Blessed

[12] Cocchi, *Commentarium,* III, n. 79.

Virgin and the Feast of All Saints.[13] The Holy See granted this petition the following year, thereby suppressing all Feastdays other than those just listed.[14]

The six Feastdays retained by the Council are all enumerated in canon 1247, § 1, and therefore continue to bind under the New Code. The four other Feastdays enumerated in the canon, however, namely the Feasts of the Epiphany, Corpus Christi, St. Joseph and SS. Peter and Paul, had been suppressed for this country by the above-mentioned response of the Sacred Congregation for the Propagation of the Faith, and therefore, by virtue of canon 1247, § 3, are not of obligation.

In passing, it may be remarked that Canada, through the Provincial Council of Quebec in 1854, asked for an arrangement of Feastdays similar to that of the United States. The Sacred Congregation granted their petition, but commanded them to retain the Feast of the Epiphany and to omit the Feast of the Assumption.[15] Hence, the status of Feastday legislation in Canada today is the same as that of the United States with the exception just noted.[16]

(c) Abrogation of Motu Proprio "Supremi Disciplinae"

A difficulty arises with regard to the prescription of canon 1247, § 3. The *Motu Proprio "Supremi Disciplinae"* of Pius X abrogated the Feasts of St. Joseph and Corpus Christi for the universal Church. The Code of Canon Law reincorporated them as Feastdays for the universal Church in canon 1247, § 1. The difficulty is this. Canon 1247, § 3, as has been pointed out above, prescribes that if any Feastday enumerated in the canon has been legitimately abolished, no innovation is to be made without first consulting the Holy See. Does this paragraph, therefore, apply to the abrogation made by the *Motu Proprio "Supremi Disciplinae"* so that in those territories where the abrogation took effect, the Feasts of St. Joseph and of Corpus Christi are now no longer of obligation?

13 *Acta et Decreta*, n. 111, pp. 57-58.

14 S. C. de Prop. Fide, resp. 31 dec. 1885—cfr. *Acta et Decreta*, pp. cv-cix.

15 S. C. de Prop. Fide, resp. 25 maii 1855—*Coll. Lac.*, III, 614, 664.

16 Augustine, *A Commentary on the New Code of Canon Law* (8 vols., Vol. VI, 2. ed., St. Louis: B. Herder, 1923), VI, 172.

This much is certain. If any territory had received a special concession from the Holy See, prior to the Code, but subsequent to the *Motu Proprio* of Pius X, to observe the two Feasts in question as days of precept, then they continue as Feastdays under the New Code. But what is to be said of those territories where no such special concession had been obtained, and where at the time of the adoption of the Code the abrogation of Pius X still remained in effect? Does the Code, by virtue of canon 1247, § 3, recognize that abrogation, so that the Feasts of St. Joseph and Corpus Christi are still not days of precept?

Some authors claim that it does. For example, Coronata claims that canon 1247, § 3, applies even to the *Motu Proprio* of Pius X. He concludes that in those territories where the abrogation of the two Feasts in question had taken effect, these feasts did not necessarily have to be observed as days of precept, because the conditions embraced under paragraph three were verified. Cocchi adopts the same opinion.[17]

It is difficult to understand how such an opinion is tenable when canon 6, 1°, is applied to this question. The *Motu Proprio "Supremi Disciplinae"* of Pius X was certainly a universal law binding the entire Church. And the abrogation of the Feastdays of St. Joseph and of Corpus Christi, as contained in it, is certainly opposed to canon 1247, § 1, which includes these Feasts as days of precept for the entire Church. Canon 6, 1°, states that all universal laws opposed to the prescriptions of the Code are abrogated. Therefore, the abrogation effected by Pope Pius X in his *Motu Proprio "Supremi Disciplinae"* was in turn abrogated by the Code, since it was opposed to the prescription of canon 1247, § 1, and the Feastdays in question began to bind anew.

It seems conclusive that the norm of canon 1247, § 3, is applicable only to those Feastdays which prior to the Code had been legitimately abrogated for a particular locality, either by the Holy See or by legitimate custom, or, in other words, by particular law. It is true that canon 6, 1°, also states that particular laws opposed to the prescriptions of the Code are abrogated. But it immediately

[17] Coronata, *De Locis et Temporibus Sacris,* n. 295, III, d.; Cocchi, *Commentarium,* III, n. 79, c.

adds "*nisi de particularibus legibus aliud expresse caveatur.*" No similar provision is made, however, with regard to universal laws. Therefore canon 1247, § 3, which expressly states otherwise with regard to the abrogation as effected by paragraph one of the same canon, can apply only to abrogations made by particular law. If it were applicable to abrogations made by pre-Code universal law as well, then the new universal law, as contained in the Code, would be powerless to institute a Feastday, and its force would be restricted solely to the abrogation of Feastdays already existing.

Vermeersch-Creusen subscribe to the opinion that the prescription of paragraph three of canon 1247 is applicable only to pre-Code particular laws resulting from concordats, indults, or legitimate custom, but not to the *Motu Proprio* of Pius X. They also state that the Pontifical Commission has strongly urged the observance of the Feasts of St. Joseph and Corpus Christi in its responses. They give no citations for the responses in question, however, and the writer has been unable to trace any of them.[18]

It is interesting to note that Vermeersch-Creusen changed their opinion on this question, having formerly held that paragraph three was applicable also to the *Motu Proprio "Supremi Disciplinae"* of Pius X.[19]

It seems necessary to conclude, therefore, on the force of the arguments given above, that the Feasts of St. Joseph and of Corpus Christi are of obligation everywhere except in those places where they had been legitimately abolished by particular law.

Article III. Present Discipline Regarding Feastdays of Particular Law

(a) Power of Local Ordinaries to Designate Feastdays

Canon 1244, § 2, formally concedes to local ordinaries the power to prescribe the observance of Feastdays for their own diocese or territory, but only *per modum actus*.

[18] Vermeersch-Creusen, *Epitome,* II, n. 559; Aertnys-Damen, *Theologia Moralis,* I, n. 504.

[19] Vermeersch-Creusen, *Summa Novi Iuris Canonici* (4. ed., Mechlinae: H. Dessain, 1921), n. 488.

Up to the time of the adoption of the Code it was not clear just what power local ordinaries enjoyed relative to the establishment of Feastdays for their own territories. The Constitution *Universa per orbem* of Urban VIII [20] certainly curtailed the power which they had enjoyed from the first centuries of the Church. As a matter of fact, this constitution most probably withdrew that power altogether, as is indicated by a response of the Sacred Congregation of Rites.[21] However, many authors claimed that this declaration of the Congregation did not have the force of universal law, and that consequently the power of bishops in this regard still obtained. No matter how this question be solved theoretically, the fact is that practically this power of the bishops was suppressed, because had they exercised it, they would have been acting contrary to the evident mind of the Church; at any event it was probably suppressed by custom.[22] Canon 1244, § 2, clears up all doubt concerning this matter, for it states that local ordinaries may exercise this power only *per modum actus*. The content of this paragraph will now be investigated.

First of all, it limits the concession of this power to local ordinaries. Therefore, according to canon 198, it is enjoyed by the residential bishop, abbot or prelate *nullius*, and their Vicar-General, the Administrator, Vicar and Prefect Apostolic, and also those who take their place according to the prescription of law, or who succeed to their rule according to the approved constitutions. The Vicar-General enjoys this power, since he is not expressly excluded in canon 1244, § 2. Major-superiors of exempt clerical religious institutes, however, are excluded, because they are not local ordinaries, and therefore they cannot designate Feastdays for their subjects even *per modum actus*.

(b) Conditions Placed on Its Legitimate Exercise

Those who enjoy this power, may exercise it to prescribe the observance of Feastdays only for their own diocese or territory. They

[20] *Fontes*, n. 226.

[21] S. R. C., *Concordiae*, 23 iun. 1703, ad 2—*Decr. Auth.*, S. R. C., n. 2113; also *Fontes*, n. 5728.

[22] Wernz, *Ius Decretalium*, III, n. 404; Vermeersch-Creusen, *Epitome*, II, n. 552; Coronata, *De Locis et Temporibus Sacris*, n. 275.

may, however, designate this observance for the entire diocese or territory, or for a particular parish or locality within the limits of the diocese or territory.[23]

Paragraph two of canon 1244 further states that they may use this power only "*per modum actus.*" The Code does not explain the precise meaning of this phrase, and therefore it is very difficult to determine the exact limitation which it places on the use of the power. It is certainly opposed to the phrase "*per modum habitus,*" but this phrase, too, has been subjected to greatly divergent interpretations on the part of authors. One may point to some examples of the widely differing interpretations which have been applied to each of these phrases.

Beste, commenting on canon 1244, § 2, writes:

> "*Per modum tantum actus,*" id est, non habitualiter multoque minus in perpetuum, sed transeunter dumtaxat ob causam transitoriam, etsi dispositio ordinarii ad plures annos protrahatur.[24]

Lehmkuhl, on the other hand, commenting on the faculty of bishops to allow Mass to be celebrated outside of a church or oratory, states:

> . . . *per modum actus, i. e.,* non habitualiter, sed pro singulis vicibus seu una alterave vice concedere possint.[25]

The phrase "*per modum habitus*" has been subjected to an equal elasticity of interpretation at the hands of authors.

Coronata writes in his commentary on canon 1244, § 2:

> . . . *per modum habitus,* seu facultati agendi pro omnibus casibus et in perpetuum.[26]

[23] Coronata, *De Locis et Temporibus Sacris,* n. 275; Vermeersch-Creusen, *Epitome,* II, n. 552.

[24] Beste, *Introductio in Codicem* (Collegeville, Minnesota: St. John's Abbey Press, 1938), p. 606.

[25] Lehmkuhl, *Theologia Moralis,* II, 167.

[26] Coronata, *De Locis et Temporibus Sacris,* n. 275, 2°, b.

Vermeersch-Creusen, however, in commenting on canon 199, § 3, state:

> . . . *habitualiter* concessa, valet pro numero casuum definito vel pro omnibus casibus per certum tempus.[27]

It is evident, therefore, that to define with any degree of certainty the exact extent of the power of local ordinaries to prescribe the observance of Feastdays for their own territories is impossible. The most that can be done is to adopt the opinion which appears the most probable. Therefore, for reasons which will be discussed at greater length in another portion of this study, namely, in the article dealing with the requisite place for the hearing of Mass, the opinion offered by the writer is this: The local ordinary can designate a Feastday for his territory, or any part of it, to be observed but once, or even two or three times in successive years, so long as he does so by distinct acts of designation. Very probably also he can designate a Feastday to be observed for two or three consecutive years by one act of designation.[28]

On the other hand, he certainly cannot designate a Feastday to be observed perpetually or for many successive years, by one and the same act, or even, most probably, by separate and distinct acts. For if he were to do so, he would seem to be acting contrary to the mind of the Code, which, by using the phrase "*per modum tantum actus*" apparently grants him very restricted power in this regard. The whole history of the bishops' power relative to the institution of Feastdays—the abuses resultant upon its use, its curtailment and probably total abolition by the Constitution *Universa per orbem* of Urban VIII—certainly lends corroboration to this conclusion. Furthermore, canon 19, which states that laws which contain an exception from the law are to be strictly interpreted, is applicable here, and demands a strict interpretation of the phrase in question.[29]

Finally, it is to be noted that canon 1244, § 2, concedes to local

[27] Vermeersch-Creusen, *Epitome,* I, n. 318.

[28] Vermeersch-Creusen, *Epitome,* II, n. 552; DeMeester, *Compendium,* n. 1240.

[29] Cf. Michiels, *Normae Generales,* I, 448-450.

ordinaries the power to *merely* designate Feastdays for their territories. Therefore, they have no power to abolish or transfer Feastdays of universal law, or even of particular law emanating from the Holy See, even *per modum actus.* Since the Code makes no other prescriptions relative to the constitution, transfer or abolition of Feastdays of particular law emanating from the Holy See, it must be concluded that the power in this regard is, in the same way as that relative to Feastdays of universal law, reserved to the supreme ecclesiastical authority, as has been stated in the first article of this chapter.

Article IV. Subjects of the Obligation Which Arises From Feastdays of Particular Law

In general, it may be said that the same qualifications are requisite for anyone to become the subject of a particular law prescribing the hearing of Mass, as are required for anyone to become the subject of the universal law, namely, that he be baptized, and that he have completed his seventh year, etc. However, since the obligation arising from Feastdays of particular law, whether prescribed by the Holy See, or by the local ordinary, is restricted to the territory for which they were designated, certain added qualifications are requisite before one becomes subject to it. It is these added qualifications which are required only in the subject of particular law, which will be considered in this article. The consideration of the qualifications commonly required in those subject to the obligation arising from Feastdays of universal law, as well as of particular law will be postponed to Chapter X of this study.

Canon 13 states:

> § 2: Legibus conditis pro peculiari territorio ii subiiciuntur pro quibus latae sunt quique ibidem domicilium vel quasi-domicilium habent et simul actu commorantur, firmo praescripto can. 14.

(a) Incolae and Advenae

Therefore, that one be subject to the obligation of a Feastday of particular law, it is necessary that he have a domicile or quasi-domicile in the territory where the observance of the Feastday is prescribed. The law relative to domicile and quasi-domicile is contained in canons 91-95. It need only be remarked here that if the Feastday is prescribed for only a particular locality within the diocese or territory of the ordinary, then, in order to be subject to the law, the person must have the domicile or quasi-domicile within that locality. He would not be obliged to hear Mass if his domicile or quasi-domicile were within the territory of the ordinary, but outside the limits of the locality for which the observance of the Feastday is prescribed.

In addition to having a domicile or quasi-domicile the person must be actually in the territory where the law binds. The obligation of fulfilling territorial laws binds only within the limits of the territory for which they were enacted. And canon 8, § 2, states that a law is presumed not to be personal, but rather territorial, unless the contrary is evident. Therefore, unless the legislator expressly states that the particular law prescribing the observance of a Feastday is a personal law, it is to be presumed a territorial law. Consequently, only those persons who are actually in the affected territory when the obligation urges are bound to fulfill it. This statement, however, demands further explanation.

It is possible that a person be in the territory even after the obligation has begun to bind and still not be obliged to hear Mass. The Feastday obligation prescribes the hearing of Mass, that is, the placing of one act. While it may be truly said that the obligation binds all during the time when the celebration of Mass is permissible, the individual subject is free to place the act fulfilling it at any time he chooses. He may attend the first Mass celebrated on the designated day, and thereby discharge his obligation, or he may attend the last Mass. Therefore, it may be said that the obligation does not begin to urge him as an individual until the time of the last Mass available to him arrives. Up to that time, he is free to postpone the fulfillment of the prescribed obligation; once that time has arrived, further postponement is impossible.

This observation is of great importance for the following reason. Any person within a territory where the observance of a Feastday is prescribed by particular law may leave that territory even on the morning of the Feastday itself, and enter a territory where the hearing of Mass is not prescribed. But he must have left the territory *before* the time of the last Mass arrives. If he has done so, he was not obliged to hear Mass before he left, because the obligation had not yet truly begun to bind him as an individual, since he could still have postponed its fulfillment, and he is not obliged to fulfill it outside the prescribed territory, because he is no longer a subject of the particular law. Furthermore, he may leave the territory as described above, precisely for the purpose of evading the law.[80]

Some few authors hold that a person is free to leave the territory as long as the complete interval during which the obligation binds has not elapsed. Thus Michiels, quoting Vermeersch, claims that a person could leave at any time *"ante prandium."* [81]

While it is true that theoretically the obligation of hearing Mass on a Feastday ceases only when the celebration of Mass is no longer permissible, practically the obligation ceases with the celebration of the latest available Mass in the affected territory. Therefore, a person who is still in the territory when the time of the last Mass arrives would be obliged to attend it, even though it be celebrated at an early hour.

The norms given above with regard to leaving a territory in which the observance of a Feastday of particular law is prescribed, are equally applicable in regard to leaving a territory where the observance of a Feastday of universal law is prescribed, if the person leaves that territory for a locality where the same law is not in effect.

(b) Vagi and Peregrini

In addition to those who have a domicile or quasi-domicile in a territory where the observance of a Feastday is prescribed by par-

[80] Marc-Gestermann, *Institutiones Morales Alphonsianae* (17. ed., 2 vols., Lugduni: Emmanuel Vitte, 1922), I, n. 207; Konings, *Theologia Moralis* (Bostoniae: Patricius Donahoe, 1874), n. 110; St. Alphonsus, *Theologia Moralis,* lib. I, n. 157; Aertnys-Damen, *Theologia Moralis,* I, n. 151; Maroto, *Institutiones Iuris Canonici* (3. ed., 2 vols., Romae: Commentarium pro Religiosis, 1921), I, n. 202, c.; Noldin-Schmitt, *De Principiis Theologiae Moralis* (20. ed., Oeniponte: Fel. Rauch, 1929), n. 152.

[81] Michiels, *Normae Generales,* I, 327, n. 1.

ticular law, and who are at the same time actually present within the territory, there are others who are obliged to hear Mass. Thus *vagi,* who according to canon 91, have no domicile or quasi-domicile in any place whatsoever, are bound by the obligation, for canon 14, § 2, states that they are bound by all laws, general as well as particular, which are in force in the place where they actually are.

Regulars and exempt religious of houses which are located in the territory are also bound to fulfill the obligation. This is evident from a prescription of the Council of Trent, which expressly states that regulars must observe Feastdays designated by the local ordinary, and which is listed in the footnotes to canon 1244, § 2, as one of the sources of the canon.[32]

It remains now only to determine the obligation of *peregrini* with regard to Feastdays of particular law. A *peregrinus* is one who has a domicile or quasi-domicile which he still retains, but who is absent from the territory in which the domicile or quasi-domicile is located.[33]

According to canon 14, § 1, 2°, a *peregrinus* is not bound by the laws of the territory in which he stays, except by those which consult the public order or which determine the solemnity of acts. A particular law prescribing a Feastday manifestly has no connection with determining the solemnity of acts. Therefore, a *peregrinus* would be bound to observe a Feastday of particular law only if it consulted the public order. While it is difficult to determine exactly just what is meant by a law "consulting the public order," it is very probable that a law which prescribes the observance of a Feastday does not fall under this category.[34] It may be safely concluded, then, that at least, in practice, a *peregrinus* is not bound by such a law. If, in any individual case, the neglect to observe a Feastday of particular law would give rise to scandal, then the *peregrinus* would be bound to observe it. The obligation here, however, would arise not from the particular law, but from the natural law.

[32] Conc. Trident., sess. XXV, *de regularibus,* c. 12; Coronata, *De Locis et Temporibus Sacris,* n. 275; DeMeester, *Compendium,* n. 1240.

[33] Canon 91.

[34] Cf. Vermeersch-Creusen, *Epitome,* I, n. 110; Cicognani, *Canon Law* (authorized English version trans. from Latin original by J. M. O'Hara and F. Brennan, Philadelphia: Dolphin Press, 1934), p. 583.

If a *peregrinus* is in a territory where a Feastday of universal law is observed, then he must fulfill the law, even if in his own territory that law is not in effect. This is clearly expressed in canon 14, § 1, 3°.

As a conclusion to this article, it may be observed that persons who leave their own territory in due time to be freed from the obligation of attending Mass there and who enter a territory where the same day is prescribed as a Feastday by particular law, need not hear Mass in either territory, for they are not actually present in their own territory when the obligation urges them as individuals, and they are *peregrini* in the territory to which they go. Therefore, they are not subject to the law of hearing Mass in either of the two territories. But if a *peregrinus* returns to his own territory in time to attend Mass on a Feastday prescribed there, he is bound to do so, because the conditions required to render him subject to the law are verified.

CHAPTER IX

PRECEPT OF HEARING MASS: ITS NATURE, GRAVITY, MATTER

Canon 1248: Festis de praecepto diebus Missa audienda est; . . .

THE Code of Canon Law in canon 1248 imposes a twofold obligation upon the faithful for the observance of Sundays and Feastdays, the one positive, namely, the hearing of Mass, and the other, negative, namely, the abstention from servile work. The present study, by reason of its restricted scope, will be concerned only with the positive obligation, namely, the hearing of Mass.

Canon 1248 merely prescribes that on Sundays and Feastdays Mass must be heard. In doing so, it simply restates the former discipline relative to this observance. Therefore, in accordance with canon 6, 2°, the precept of hearing Mass as obligatory today is to be estimated according to the interpretations of approved authors. The nature and gravity of the obligation, its matter, and the causes which excuse from its fulfillment, etc., are to be determined according to the teaching of recognized canonists and theologians who wrote before the Code. Post-Code authors have followed out this prescription of canon 6, 2°, and accordingly have adopted, with some few exceptions, the opinions of pre-Code authors.

One exception may be found in canon 1249 which makes a special provision as to the place where the obligation of hearing Mass may be legitimately fulfilled. The prescription contained in this canon differs from the old law, and therefore requires special interpretation. A special chapter of this study will be devoted to a consideration of that matter.

The present chapter will confine itself to an investigation of the precept itself—its gravity and its matter—and the obligation of the faithful arising therefrom.

Article I. Nature and Gravity of the Precept

The precept of hearing Mass is a merely ecclesiastical positive law which prescribes a personal act for the performance of which a certain time is assigned *ad finiendam obligationem*. By this is meant that the obligation binds only on the Sunday or Feastday itself, and that once the Sunday or Feastday has passed, the obligation ceases. Therefore the precept of hearing Mass can be fulfilled only on the day designated; it cannot be anticipated nor can it be supplied on a later day.[1]

It imposes upon the faithful a grave obligation, as is evident from the proposition condemned by Pope Innocent XI (1676-1689) which reads:

> Praeceptum servandi festa non obligat sub mortali, seposito scandalo, si absit contemptus.[2]

Moreover, its gravity stands attested by the common consent of the faithful and the unanimous teaching of theologians both before and after the Code.[3]

Certain authors, according to St. Alphonsus, ventured the opinion that the neglect of hearing Mass on one or the other Feastday during the year would constitute only light matter, and therefore entail the commission of no more than venial sin. St. Alphonsus himself rejects this opinion on the grounds that it was expressly reprobated by the condemnation of Innocent XI quoted above.[4]

Since the obligation under grave sin arising from the precept of hearing Mass is not a general one, but a specific obligation attached to each individual Sunday and Feastday, it is difficult to see what

[1] Noldin-Schmitt, *De Principiis*, n. 174; Marc-Gestermann, *Institutiones Morales*, I, n. 213, and practically all others.

[2] Prop. 52—Denzinger-Bannwart-Umberg, *Enchiridion Symbolorum, Definitionum, et Declarationum de Rebus Fidei et Morum* (ed. 22-23, Friburgi Brisgoviae: Herder, 1937), n. 1202. Hereafter cited as Denzinger-Bannwart.

[3] St. Alphonsus, *Theologia Moralis*, lib. III, n. 268; Wernz, *Ius Decretalium*, III, n. 405; DeMeester, *Compendium*, n. 1246; Coronata, *De Locis et Temporibus Sacris*, n. 289; Aertnys-Damen, *Theologia Moralis*, I, n. 505.

[4] *Op. cit.*, lib. III, n. 308.

possible grounds there are on which to base this opinion. Most of the authors do not even consider this question, and since in many individual cases it could become vastly important, it may be reasonably presumed that they reject it as having little, if any probability. Therefore it may be considered as totally untenable.

It must not be deduced from this, however, that the precept admits of no light matter whatsoever. The neglect of fulfilling its prescription constitutes a sin *mortale ex genere suo,* and therefore does admit of light matter. The light matter would consist, however, not in the occasional omission of an entire Mass, but in the omission of a portion of the Mass. Just how great an omission can be regarded as light matter will be discussed in the next article of this chapter.

If a Sunday and Feastday should coincide, the obligation of hearing Mass may be fulfilled by hearing only one Mass. A person, therefore, who neglects to hear Mass on such a day commits but one mortal sin. The reason is that while the person may truly be considered to be obligated by two precepts—one by reason of the Sunday, and the other by reason of the Feastday—these precepts are not formally distinct, since they prescribe the same matter, and prescribe it for the same purpose, namely, the sanctification of the day.[5]

It is clear from canon 1248 that the positive element of the precept of sanctifying Sundays and Feastdays consists solely in the hearing of Mass. There is no precept obliging the faithful to attend Vespers, to be present at sermons or to assist at other religious services. Therefore, even if a person misses Mass, he cannot be bound as a matter of obligation to supply for the omission by the recitation of prayers, or by attendance at other religious functions.

In some cases an individual may be obliged to attend services other than the Mass, such as sermons and instructions, if such be necessary for his salvation. Here, however, the obligation would arise, not from the Sunday and Feastday precept, but from the natural law, for one who is bound to attain an end, is obliged to use the means necessary for its attainment.[6]

[5] Aertnys-Damen, *Theologia Moralis,* I, n. 224; Noldin-Schmitt, *De Principiis,* n. 172; St. Alphonsus, *Theologia Moralis,* lib. I, n. 167.

[6] Iorio, *Theologia Moralis,* II, n. 124.

ARTICLE II. THE MATTER OF THE PRECEPT OF HEARING MASS

(a) Obligation to Hear Entire Mass

As has been stated before, the Code in canon 1248 contents itself with stating merely that on Sundays and Feastdays Mass must be heard. To determine more precisely what obligations are engendered by this general prescription of canon 1248, it is necessary to examine the opinions of recognized authors.

It is the common teaching of authors that the precept of hearing Mass binds to the hearing of an entire Mass. Therefore the matter of the precept as contained in canon 1248 consists in the hearing, not only of the substance of the Mass, which includes only the essential and integral parts of the sacrifice as instituted by Christ, namely, the twofold Consecration and the Communion, but also of the accidental portion of the Mass, which includes all other parts from the beginning of the Mass to the *Ite Missa Est* inclusively.[7]

Some authors include even the Last Gospel as part of the matter of the precept, claiming that, while it is something superadded, it is nevertheless a part of the liturgy, and therefore obligatory.[8] It seems more probable, however, that the Last Gospel does not pertain to the matter of the precept, since through the words *Ite Missa Est* the faithful are dismissed.[9]

Strictly speaking, the precept binds to the hearing of one integral Mass, that is, the hearing of all the parts of one and the same Mass. Therefore, it would not suffice that a person hear different parts of two or more Masses celebrated simultaneously, as is evident from the proposition condemned by Pope Innocent XI, which reads:

[7] St. Alphonsus, *Theologia Moralis,* lib. III, n. 310; Wernz, *Ius Decretalium,* III, n. 406; Gasparri, *De Sanctissima Eucharistia,* II, n. 956; Aertnys-Damen, *Theologia Moralis,* I, n. 520; Marc-Gestermann, *Institutiones,* I, n. 672; Merkelbach, *Summa Theologiae Moralis,* II, n. 699.

[8] Coronata, *De Locis et Temporibus Sacris,* n. 289; Gasparri, *loc. cit.*

[9] St. Alphonsus, *Homo Apostolicus,* tr. VI, n. 33; Aertnys-Damen, *Theologia Moralis,* I, n. 521; Marc-Gestermann, *Institutiones,* I, n. 672; Merkelbach, *Summa,* II, n. 699; Iorio, *Theologia Moralis,* II, n. 128.

Satisfacit praecepto Ecclesiae de audiendo Sacro qui duas partes, imo quatuor simul diversis celebrantibus audit.[10]

However, it is the common teaching of authors that the precept may be fulfilled by the hearing of different parts of two Masses celebrated successively, provided that the twofold Consecration and the Communion form part of one and the same Mass. The reason advanced in support of this opinion is that when the Consecration and Communion are united in one and the same Mass a complete and perfect Sacrifice is attended. It is hardly to be presumed, therefore, that the Church would prohibit *sub gravi* the supplying from another Mass of the minor and accidental parts which were not heard during the essential sacrifice.[11] However, one, who for no reason whatsoever would discharge his obligation in this manner, could hardly be excused from venial sin.

Some few authors, among them Coronata,[12] prepose as probable the opinion that the precept of hearing Mass can be fulfilled by the assistance at different parts of successive Masses even when the Consecration and Communion are not contained in one and the same Mass. St. Alphonsus rejects this opinion, stating that it is not sufficiently probable and that the precept cannot be fulfilled in this manner. The reason he alleges is this: The Church prescribes the hearing of a Mass, which is a single integral sacrifice. And one who hears half-parts of two successive Masses, one of which contains the Consecration and the other, the Communion, cannot be said to assist at one perfect sacrifice. He assists, rather, at two imperfect sacrifices, and does not, therefore, fulfill the precept of the Church.[13]

(b) Grave and Light Matter in Omissions

It has already been stated in the first article of this chapter that the precept of hearing Mass binds under mortal sin *ex genere suo*

[10] Prop. 53—Denzinger-Bannwart, n. 1203.

[11] St. Alphonsus, *Theologia Moralis*, lib. III, n. 311; and almost all others.

[12] *De Locis et Temporibus Sacris*, n. 289.

[13] *Theologia Moralis*, lib. III, n. 311.

and therefore admits of light matter. It will be appropriate here to consider the various parts of Mass the voluntary omission of which constitutes a grave sin, and those parts the voluntary omission of which constitutes a venial sin.

It is commonly taught by theologians that the omission of one-third of the Mass suffices to constitute grave matter. Some authors observe that it is difficult to estimate precisely just how much of the Mass constitutes one-third, because in determining it one must take into consideration not only the duration of time, but also the inherent dignity and relative importance of the parts concerned.[14] It seems, however, that since one-third of any given object is of its very nature purely quantitative, the determination of one-third of the Mass should be based solely on its quantitative relation to the whole Mass.

The observation of the authors just cited, nevertheless, is correct in so far as the dignity and rělative importance of the parts concerned must be taken into consideration, not indeed, to determine a third-part of the Mass, but rather to determine the gravity or lightness of the omission. Therefore it is better to state, with Aertnys-Damen, that a twofold norm must be used for determining whether any given omission constitutes grave or only light matter, the one quantitative, looking to the quantity of the part omitted, and the other qualitative, looking to the dignity and importance of the part concerned.[15]

This twofold norm will be applied in the conclusions which follow. First will be enumerated those omissions which are grave or light in view of their quantitative aspects; then those which are grave or light by reason of their qualitative aspect. Since authors are at variance on almost every specific application of the twofold general norm, and it would be almost impossible as well as impractical to list all the offered opinions, the conclusions which follow represent the opinions which, to the mind of the writer, seem most probable.

The following omissions, estimated in view of their quantitative character, constitute GRAVE matter:

[14] Iorio, *Theologia Moralis,* II, n. 128; Merkelbach, *Summa,* II, n. 700.

[15] Aertnys-Damen, *Theologia Moralis,* I, n. 521.

(1) The beginning of the Mass to the offertory inclusive. St. Alphonsus [16] regarded as more probable that opinion which would include under grave matter that omission which comprises from the beginning of the Mass to the Epistle inclusive. But he admitted the probability of the other opinion. Today the more lenient opinion is reflected in the common teaching of authors as well as in the common conviction of the faithful.[17]

(2) The Communion of the Mass with what follows. This is the common opinion.

(3) All the parts before the Gospel together with all the parts after the Communion. This is also the common teaching.

(4) The Offertory up to and including a part of the Canon.[18]

It is evident that the parts of the Mass indicated above as constituting grave matter do not constitute a quantitative third of the Mass with mathematical exactness. If mathematical exactness were demanded then the estimation of one-third of the Mass would have to be adjusted to fit each individual Mass, and would vary in accordance with the length of the proper parts, the recitation or non-recitation of the *Gloria* and *Credo,* etc. Therefore the opinions necessarily represent only a moral estimation of a quantitative third.

The following omissions, as deduced from the above opinions, constitute LIGHT matter:

(1) The parts following the Communion.

(2) All the parts before the Epistle together with all the parts after the Communion.

(3) The beginning of the Mass to the *Credo* inclusive.

(4) The Offertory to the Preface inclusive.

In connection with the application of the qualitative norm it is necessary to state that the dignity and importance of the individual parts of the Mass increase in proportion to their proximity to the Consecration. This consideration, as well as the consideration of the

[16] *Theologia Moralis,* lib. III, n. 310.

[17] Marc-Gestermann, *Institutiones,* I, n. 672; Iorio, *Theologia Moralis,* II, n. 128; Merkelbach, *Summa,* II, n. 700.

[18] Merkelbach, *loc. cit.;* Iorio, *loc. cit.*

inherent dignity of the individual parts themselves, has been taken into account in the specific application which follows.[19]

By reason of the qualitative norm, therefore, the following omissions are GRAVE:

(1) Either Consecration, and, *a fortiori,* both Consecrations (Iorio, Aertnys-Damen, Merkelbach, Marc-Gestermann and others). St. Alphonsus [20] holds this opinion, although he admits as probable the opinion that the omission of the Consecration would not in itself be grave. Since the twofold Consecration constitutes the entire essence of the Mass, or at least pertains to the essence, it seems that its omission necessarily constitutes grave matter, because in the event of such an omission a true Mass would not be heard.

(2) The Communion alone (Aertnys-Damen, Merkelbach, Marc-Gestermann). This omission seems grave because the Communion possibly pertains to the essence of the sacrifice, and certainly forms at least an integral part of the sacrifice as instituted by Christ. Therefore it is a part notable in dignity and importance. Its omission destroys the integrity of the Mass as Christ instituted it, and for this reason constitutes in all probability grave matter.

(3) From the Preface to the Consecration exclusive (Gasparri).

(4) From the Consecration to the *Pater Noster* exclusive (Aertnys-Damen, St. Alphonsus).

The opinions given under numbers 3 and 4 are drawn from the application of both the quantitative and the qualitative norms. The relative length of the parts in addition to their dignity and importance as proximate to the Consecration seems to justify their classification as grave matter.

The following omissions would be LIGHT:

(1) The Offertory alone (Merkelbach). For while it is one of the principal parts of the Mass, its dignity and importance do not seem sufficient to render its omission grave.

(2) The parts of the Canon smaller than those indicated above.

[19] Gasparri, *De Sanctissima Eucharistia,* II, n. 958; Coronata, *De Locis et Temporibus Sacris,* n. 289.

[20] *Homo Apostolicus,* tr. VI, n. 33; *Theologia Moralis,* lib. III, n. 310.

Article III. Obligation to Supply Omitted Parts of Mass

(a) *Obligation When Grave Matter Is Omitted*

It has been pointed out that the precept binds to the hearing of an entire Mass from its beginning to its end at the blessing of the priest. Since an omission, however small, of any part of the Mass renders the fulfillment of the precept incomplete, it follows logically that an obligation rests upon the faithful to supply from another Mass those parts which have been omitted.

It is very important to note that this obligation to supply exists when the omission has been inculpable as well as when it has been culpable. The only difference lies in the fact that if the person is unable to supply the omitted parts, he would be guilty of sin in proportion to his fault if the omission has been culpable, but guilty of no sin at all if the omission has been inculpable.

All authors agree that there is an obligation *sub gravi* to supply those omitted parts of Mass which constitute grave matter. It goes without saying that if the supplying of these parts would involve notable harm or inconvenience, the obligation would cease. In other words the same excusing causes which release one from the obligation of hearing Mass also release one from the obligation of supplying inculpably omitted parts. If the omission of any part were culpable then the person would be obliged to supply the omitted parts even at the cost of notable inconvenience, and in the event that the necessary supplying is impossible, he would be guilty of sin in proportion to his fault.

It may be stated in general that it is sufficient to supply from another Mass only those parts which have been omitted in the first. In the application of this rule, however, it must be kept in mind that the Consecration and Communion must be contained in one and the same Mass. Hence, a person who has missed the Consecration of the first Mass would not fulfill his obligation by merely attending the Consecration of the second; he must attend both the Consecration and the Communion of the second.

(b) *Obligation When Light Matter Is Omitted*

Authors disagree as to whether there is an obligation to supply omitted parts which constitute only light matter. Some deny that there is such an obligation. They contend that the precept has already been substantially fulfilled, and that therefore no further obligation remains, because "*res morales non sunt adeo rigorose expendendae, praesertim quando leviores sunt. . . .*"[21]

The more probable opinion, however, and the more logical one, is that even those omitted parts which constitute only light matter must be supplied under pain of venial sin. The precept binds to the hearing of an entire Mass. If the omission of grave matter gives rise to an obligation to supply *sub gravi,* it seems only reasonable to conclude that the omission of light matter gives rise to a similar obligation *sub levi.* If the omission was very slight, it may be dismissed as negligible. It is to be noted that a reason proportionate to the omission in question will excuse from the obligation of supplying, provided the omission was inculpable.[22]

(c) Obligation If Not All of the Mass Can Be Heard

Before this chapter is brought to a conclusion, another question relevant to the matter under consideration must be answered. The question is this: What is the obligation of those who arrive late for Mass, and who cannot hear another Mass. Must they stay for the parts of the Mass which still remain?

Practically all authors without exception admit that if the person arrives BEFORE the Consecration, he is bound to assist at the part remaining, because he can still fulfill the substance of the precept. If he arrives AFTER the Consecration, however, authors dissent as to his obligation to remain for the rest of the Mass. Some hold that he is under no obligation to do so, because he can no longer fulfill the substance of the precept.[23]

[21] Suarez, *De Eucharistia,* disp. 88, sect. 2; Vermeersch, *Theologia Moralis,* III, n. 860.

[22] St. Alphonsus, *Theologia Moralis,* lib. III, n. 310; Gasparri, *De Sanctissima Eucharistia,* II, n. 957, and many others.

[23] Vermeersch, *Theologia Moralis,* III, n. 860; Merkelbach, *Summa,* II, n. 700; Iorio, *Theologia Moralis,* II, n. 129; Gasparri, *De Sanctissima Eucharistia,* II, n. 960.

The better opinion seems to be that those who come after the Consecration are bound to remain for the rest of the Mass. The reason that the Church prescribes the hearing of an entire Mass, and therefore those who cannot fulfill the precept in its entirety, are bound to fulfill as much of it as is in their power.[24]

[24] St. Alphonsus, *Theologia Moralis,* lib. III, n. 310; Aertnys-Damen, *Theologia Moralis,* I, n. 522; Prümmer, *Manuale Theologiae Moralis,* II, n. 479; and others.

CHAPTER X

SUBJECT OF THE PRECEPT OF HEARING MASS

THE preceding chapter dealt with the matter of the precept of hearing Mass on Sundays and Feastdays, namely, with what is prescribed by the law. It is the purpose of the present chapter to investigate the subject of the precept, namely, who is bound to observe it, and what is demanded of him in order that he fulfill the obligation.

ARTICLE I. THE SUBJECT OF THE PRECEPT OF HEARING MASS

Canon 12: Legibus mere ecclesiasticis non tenentur qui baptismum non receperunt, nec baptizati qui sufficienti rationis usu non gaudent, nec qui, licet rationis usum assecuti, septimum aetatis annum nondum expleverunt, nisi aliud iure expresse caveatur.

(a) Subject in General

The precept of hearing Mass on Sundays and Feastdays is a merely ecclesiastical law. Since the Code makes no special provisions regarding the subject of the precept, the subject is to be determined by application of the rule of canon 12. This canon enumerates those who are not bound by ecclesiastical laws, namely, the unbaptized, the baptized who do not enjoy a sufficient use of reason, and those baptized who, while they enjoy the use of reason, have not completed their seventh year of age. By deduction, therefore, it may be stated that the subject of the precept of hearing Mass must be baptized, must enjoy a sufficient use of reason, and must have completed his seventh year. It will be profitable to consider each of these requisites in order.

The subject must be baptized: By this is meant that he must have received valid baptism of water. The reason baptism is necessary in order that a person become subject to the laws of the Church, is that by baptism he is constituted a member of the Church with all the obligations attendant upon that membership.[1] Hence, infidels, Jews, and catechumens are not directly bound by merely ecclesiastical laws for they are not members of the ecclesiastical society for whom alone the Church can directly legislate.[2]

Since the Code does not specify baptism in the Catholic Church, it follows that any baptism of water, validly received, suffices to verify the first condition required in a subject of merely ecclesiastical laws.[3]

Regarding the doubtfully baptized as subject to the law a distinction must be made. If the fact of baptism itself is certain, that is, if the external rite has been performed, and only its validity is doubted, then the person is to be considered as bound by the precept of hearing Mass on the basis of the principle *in dubio omne factum praesumitur recte factum.* If, however, the doubt centers on the fact of baptism itself, that is, if it is doubted whether the external rite was ever performed, then the person is not considered as subject to the law, because *factum in dubio non praesumitur, sed probari debet.*[4]

The subject must enjoy a sufficient use of reason. This is required because the law induces a moral obligation, and unless a person has sufficient use of reason to perceive the moral obligation and to fulfill it in a human manner, he cannot be a subject of the law.[5] Therefore the precept of hearing Mass does not include as subjects infants, the perpetually demented, or even the habitually demented who have lucid intervals, because according to canon 88, § 3, they are to be regarded as infants. Those who habitually possess the use

[1] Canon 87.

[2] Michiels, *Normae Generales,* I, 283.

[3] Vermeersch-Creusen, *Epitome,* I, n. 206; and all others.

[4] Michiels, *Normae Generales,* I, 284-285; Aertnys-Damen, *Theologia Moralis,* I, n. 148.

[5] Tanquerey, *Synopsis Theologiae Moralis et Pastoralis* (3 vols., Vols. I and III, 10. ed., Vol. II, 9. ed., Parisiis: Desclée et Socii, 1925-1936), II (1931), n. 299.

of reason, but lose it on occasion, are habitually subject to the precept, but are not bound by it on those occasions when *de facto* they are deprived of the use of their reason.[6]

It is important to note that according to canon 88, § 3, those who have completed their seventh year are presumed to have the use of reason, and therefore are bound by the precept unless the lack of the use of reason is proved.

Finally, the subject must have completed his seventh year of age. According to the norm given in canon 34, § 3, 3°, the seventh year of age is completed with the expiration of the seventh birthday anniversary and the precept of hearing Mass begins to bind only on the day after this anniversary.

It need hardly be said that the three conditions must all be realized in the same person before he becomes subject to the precept. Therefore a child who has completed his seventh year without as yet having attained a sufficient use of reason is still free from the obligation, as is also a child who has attained the use of reason but has not as yet completed his seventh year.

Whether all the persons in whom are realized the three conditions enumerated in canon 12 are bound by the precept of hearing Mass is disputed. Some authors claim that all such persons are bound. Others make an exception with regard to certain classes of the validly baptized who are not, in the strict sense, full members of the Catholic Church, namely, heretics, schismatics, excommunicates and the interdicted. This disputed question is important enough to warrant special consideration.

(b) Heretics and Schismatics

Merely ecclesiastical laws may be divided into two kinds: those which directly pertain to the public order or the common good, such as invalidating or incapacitating laws, and those which directly pertain to the personal sanctification of the individual, such as laws

[6] Michiels, *Normae Generales*, I, 292; Tanquerey, *Synopsis Theologiae Moralis et Pastoralis*, II, n. 299.

which prescribe fast and abstinence, etc. The precept of hearing Mass is of the latter type.

It is beyond question that laws which directly pertain to the public order or common good bind all the baptized without exception, unless the Church expressly exempts one or the other class in a particular instance, as she does in canon 1099, § 2, which releases non-Catholics from the required form of marriage.[7]

With almost equal certainty it can be stated that even laws which directly pertain to the personal sanctification of the individual bind all heretics and schismatics who were born and reared in the Catholic Church, or who were converted to it, and then subsequently fell away.[8]

The dispute arises, however, with regard to those baptized persons who were born and reared in heresy or schism, or who have adhered to an heretical or schismatic sect for a long time without ever having been affiliated with the Catholic Church. Are such persons bound by merely ecclesiastical laws which directly pertain to the sanctification of the individual? Certainly many of them, through lack of knowledge and good faith, commit no formal sin in transgressing such laws. But does the Church intend to exempt them from the obligation in such a way that they commit not even a material sin?

Not a few authors maintain that such is the Church's intent. Admitting that such persons through baptism become in principle subject to all the laws of the Church, they claim nevertheless that the Church exempts them from those laws which pertain directly to the sanctification of the individual. They base this opinion on a benign interpretation of the mind of the legislator, in consequence of which they maintain that the Church would not wish unduly to multiply material sins by holding such persons to an obligation which, it is foreseen, they will almost invariably disregard. For, according to their contention, the enforcement of such laws with re-

[7] Wernz, *Ius Decretalium,* I, n. 103, footnote 79; Chelodi, *Ius de Personis iuxta Codicem Iuris Canonici* (3. ed., Tridenti: Libr. Edit. Tridentum, 1921), n. 37; Maroto, *Institutiones Iuris Canonici,* I, n. 196; Noldin-Schmitt, *De Principiis,* n. 148; Vermeersch-Creusen, *Epitome,* I, n. 106.

[8] Cf. authors cited above.

gard to persons of this class would result rather in the destruction of the law than in the attainment of its purpose.[9]

This opinion, on the evaluation of the arguments adduced in support of it, seems devoid of any great probability. It rests solely on a gratuitous assumption of what the legislator intends to do, namely, that lest material sins be unduly multiplied and the purpose of the law be destroyed rather than attained, the Church intends to exempt the heretics and schismatics in question. The validity of this assumption can be gravely questioned.

First of all, what real harm would her law suffer, if the Church were to permit the multiplication of *material* sins? Just how would the purpose of the law be destroyed rather than attained? If a question of the divine law, natural or positive, were involved, or if formal sin were committed, then the harm arising out of the transgression of the law would be evident. But since it is a question of merely ecclesiastical law, the transgression of which directly affects only the transgressor, inasmuch as the law is directly intended for his own personal sanctification, how would even a widespread non-observance of the law among those who are unaware of their obligation to observe it inflict any real harm upon it? The multiplication of material sins does not destroy the purpose of the law, for *de facto* its purpose is attained in the personal sanctification of all those who actually observe it.[10] The assumption that the Church intends to exempt such heretics and schismatics seems, therefore, entirely unwarranted, and the opinion based upon it appears hardly probable. When the arguments adduced in support of the opposite opinion, namely, that the aforesaid heretics are bound by such laws, are taken into consideration, then it becomes even more difficult to acknowledge the probability of the opinion in question.

[9] Cavagnis, *Institutiones Iuris Publici Ecclesiae* (4. ed., 3 vols., Romae: Desclée, Lefebvre et Soc., 1906), I, 564; Lehmkuhl, *Theologia Moralis,* I, n. 228; Marc-Gestermann, *Institutiones Moralis,* I, n. 198; Maroto, *Institutiones Iuris Canonici,* I, n. 196; Iorio, *Theologia Moralis,* I, n. 127, 5°; Sabetti-Barrett, *Compendium Theologiae Moralis* (8. ed. post Codicem, Neo-Eboraci: Frederick Pustet, 1939), n. 78, 4°; Davis, *Moral and Pastoral Theology* (3. ed., 4 vols., New York: Sheed & Ward, 1938), I, 160.

[10] Wernz, *Ius Decretalium,* I, 124, footnote 80; Aertnys-Damen, *Theologia Moralis,* I, n. 148.

Authors who oppose the view considered above hold that even the baptized who have been born and reared in a non-Catholic sect, or who have never belonged to the Catholic Church, are nevertheless bound by all the laws of the Church, including those which pertain directly to the sanctification of the individual. In other words, such persons are exempt only when the Church expressly exempts them. Strong reasons can be adduced in support of this opinion.

First of all, the Code in canon 87 states expressly that by baptism a person is constituted a member of the Church of Christ and assumes all the duties attendant upon that membership. In canon 12 the Code states that the non-baptized are not bound by merely ecclesiastical laws, thereby clearly implying that the baptized are bound. It makes no distinction between different kinds of laws; therefore it is to be presumed that it means all laws without exception.

Secondly, the Church expressly exempts non-Catholics from certain of her laws, as for example, in canon 1099, § 2. Why then does the Church not *expressly* exempt heretics and schismatics of the type here in question from laws which pertain directly to personal sanctification, if it intends to exempt them at all? Surely the Church is aware of the widespread disregard of such laws and the resultant multiplication of material sins. If *de facto* this universal disregard among non-Catholics and the material sins resultant upon it are destructive of the Church's laws, why does it allow the destruction to continue?

Furthermore, it is the policy of the Church, in the external forum at least, to assume that all heretics and schismatics are formal. This may be deduced from canon 2314, § 1, which, in enumerating the penalties inflicted upon heretics and schismatics, uses the words "*omnes et singuli haeretici aut schismatici.*" It would be difficult to reconcile with this policy the opinion that the Church intends to exempt the greater number of heretics and schismatics from certain of her laws and thereby seemingly attach a benefit to their separation.

It can hardly be questioned that, due to the clear and express statements of canons 12 and 87 to the effect that all baptized persons are bound by all ecclesiastical laws, the opinion favoring exemption enjoys less probability today than it did before the Code was adopted. And yet, the great majority of the authors who wrote before the

Code rejected this opinion, and maintained that all the baptized were bound by all the Church's laws.[11]

In addition to this certain documents emanating from the Holy See greatly weakened the opinion favoring exemption. Pope Benedict XIV in his Brief *"Singulare Nobis"* (1749) stated expressly that baptized non-Catholics were subject to all the laws of the Church.[12] Likewise the Congregation for the Propagation of the Faith in two responses indicated at least indirectly that baptized non-Catholics are bound even by the laws that pertain to personal sanctification, when it allowed Catholics to co-operate materially in the breaking of such laws by non-Catholics only when their refusal to do so would cause the Catholics grave detriment.[13]

The force of these two responses as an argument against exemption would no doubt not be acknowledged by the proponents of the opinion which favors exemption. For practically all of them, on the testimony of Maroto, admit that very limitation; for they conclude:

> Ex eo tamen quod haeretici hisce legibus non teneantur non licet inferre catholicos eis legum violationem suadere vel iniungere posse, quia Ecclesia non permittit ut a catholicis ad agendum contra legem inducantur.[14]

This conclusion, however, seems strangely inconsistent with the opinion which they support. They claim on the one hand that the non-Catholics in question are exempt from the law, and on the other hand they assert that Catholics are not allowed to induce them to act against the law. If they offer this conclusion as one to be followed in view of the probability of the opinion that such non-Catholics are bound, then it offers no difficulty. But if they offer it as a conclusion which follows from their own opinion, which they seem to

[11] Cf. *e.g.*, Reiffenstuel, *Ius Canonicum Universum* (7 vols., Parisiis: 1864-1870), lib. I, tit. 2, n. 274; Suarez, *De Legibus*, lib. IV, c. 19, n. 2. Cf. also Michiels, *Normae Generales*, I, 289.

[12] Benedictus XIV, ep. *"Singulare Nobis,"* 9 febr. 1749, §§ 12, 16—*Fontes*, n. 394.

[13] S. C. de Prop. Fide responsa, 26 iun. 1820—*Coll. S. C. de Prop. Fide*, nn. 747, 748.

[14] Maroto, *Institutiones Iuris Canonici*, I, n. 196.

do, then it seems hardly logical. For how can a person act contrary to a law by which he is not bound? What possible guilt could be attributed to a Catholic who assisted such non-Catholics to do something which they are entirely free to do, or who induced them to omit placing an act which they were under no obligation to place. The prohibition which is placed upon Catholics seems logical only when the opinion is held that the non-Catholics are *de facto* bound by the laws in question. Therefore the argument drawn above from the responses of the Congregation seems valid and strongly corroborative of the opinion which contends that all baptized non-Catholics are subject to even those laws of the Church which pertain directly to personal sanctification.

In evaluating the two opinions discussed above merely on the basis of the arguments adduced in support of them, the present writer holds that the opinion which avers the subjection of all baptized non-Catholics to all the laws of the Church is the only intrinsically probable opinion, and that the one which favors their exemption is intrinsically improbable. But besides having far greater intrinsic probability the opinion favoring the obligation of all heretics and schismatics to observe all the Church's laws, unless in a particular case an express exception is made, also enjoys the support of the greater number of authors who have written since the Code.[15]

Applying this opinion to the specific subject of the present study, the writer unhesitatingly asserts as his conviction that the precept of hearing Mass binds all heretics and schismatics, including those who were born and reared outside the Church. In view, however, of the extrinsic probability which the more benign opinion enjoys, adopted as it is by a number of recognized authors, and in view also of the possibility that heretics and schismatics born and reared outside the

[15] Wernz-Vidal, *Ius Canonicum* (7 vols. in 8, Romae: Universitas Gregoriana, 1923-1938), II, n. 1; Van Hove, *De Legibus Ecclesiasticis* (Mechlinae: H. Dessain, 1930), n. 193; Michiels, *Normae Generales,* I, 289; Noldin-Schmitt, *De Principiis,* n. 148; Aertnys-Damen, *Theologia Moralis,* I, n. 148; Chelodi, *Ius De Personis,* nn. 37, 64, n. 1; Vermeersch-Creusen, *Epitome,* I, n. 78; Wouters, *Manuale Theologiae Moralis* (2 vols., Brugis [Belgii]: Carolus Beyaert, 1932), I, 89; De Meester, *Compendium,* I, n. 310; Tanquerey, *Synopsis Theologiae Moralis,* II, n. 298.

Catholic Church have become freed of their obligation by legitimate contrary custom, he hesitates to condemn absolutely the use of this milder opinion in practice.

(c) *Excommunicates and the Interdicted*

Another controverted question relative to the precept of hearing Mass is this: Are excommunicates bound to attend Mass on Sundays and Feastdays? An adequate answer to this question can be ascertained only through the consideration of three other important questions. (1) Does the censure of excommunication merely deprive the delinquent of the RIGHT to assist at Mass, or does it at the same time impose a prohibition to do so? (2) If it imposes a prohibition, does this prohibition necessarily delete the obligation of hearing Mass? (3) If the obligation endures in spite of the prohibition, is the excommunicate bound to remove the censure in order to fulfill the precept of hearing Mass? These questions will be considered in order.

(1) It is clear from canon 2259, § 1, which states: *Excommunicatus quilibet caret iure assistendi divinis officiis, non tamen praedicationi verbi Dei,* that all excommunicates without exception are deprived of the RIGHT to assist at Mass. Is this deprivation of the RIGHT tantamount to a prohibition to assist? Some authors maintain that it is, and that consequently all excommunicates are forbidden to assist at the Holy Sacrifice.[16] These authors offer no argumentation in support of their claim. Perhaps they reason to their conclusion as follows: All the faithful have the right to assist at Mass on Sundays and Feastdays and other days. They are obliged to exercise that right on certain days prescribed by the Church. Canon 2259, § 1, deprives excommunicates of the right to assist at Mass, and therefore the exercise of that right is prohibited to them with the result that the obligation to hear Mass on Sundays and Feastdays ceases.

16 Chelodi-Dalpiaz, *Ius Poenale et Ordo Procedendi in Iudiciis Criminalibus iuxta Codicem Iuris Canonici* (4. ed., Tridenti: Libreria Moderna Editrice A. Ardesi, 1935), n. 37; Cappello, *Tractatus Canonico-Moralis de Censuris iuxta Codicem Iuris Canonici* (2. ed., Taurinorum-Augustae: Marietti, 1925), n. 149; and others.

It is the opinion of the present writer that canon 2259, § 1, does not prohibit excommunicates from assisting at Mass. It is true that under the old law all excommunicates without exception were forbidden to attend the divine offices.[17] In the course of time, however, custom introduced a more lenient attitude toward the *tolerati,* and some theologians ventured the opinion that these were no longer prohibited from assisting at these offices.[18] This opinion did not find favor with all authors. Some admitted that the prohibition placed upon *tolerati* had indeed become less severe, but they insisted that it remained a prohibition nevertheless.[19]

The Code, in canon 2259, § 1, seems to canonize the opinion which maintains that *tolerati* are not forbidden to attend divine offices. That *vitandi* are still forbidden, by reason of canon 2259, § 2, will be demonstrated subsequently. Hence the following argumentation applies exclusively to the *tolerati.*

In order to appreciate the force of the arguments which follow a clear understanding must be had of the precise nature of a RIGHT. A right may be defined as a legitimate inviolable faculty of possessing or doing something, or of demanding something as one's own.[20] It is to be clearly distinguished from the mere liceity of performing a certain act. A person may licitly perform certain acts which he has no strict right to perform. To illustrate: By virtue of canon 1188, § 2, 1°, all the faithful have a legitimately established right of entering a public oratory, at least at the time of the divine offices. By reason of this right they can legitimately demand that they be not impeded or prevented from entering the oratory when the divine offices are in progress. There is a corresponding obligation on the part of others, therefore, to respect that right and not to interfere with its exercise. The faithful enjoy no such right, however, with regard to semi-public oratories, as can be deduced from canon 1188, § 2, 2°.

[17] C. 57, X, *de sententia excommunicationis,* V. 39; c. 17, X, *de verborum significatione,* V. 40.

[18] D'Annibale, *Summula Theologiae Moralis* (3. ed., 3 vols., Romae, 1888), I, n. 362, nota 19; Bucceroni, *Commentarium de Censuris* (Romae, 1885), n. 99.

[19] *E. g.,* Lehmkuhl, *Theologia Moralis,* II, 638, n. 4.

[20] Michiels, *Normae Generales,* I, 5: *Facultas legitima inviolabilis aliquid possidendi, agendi, vel exigendi ut rigorose suum.*

But this does not imply that they may not licitly enter semi-public oratories, or that they are forbidden to do so. It means simply that if those for whose convenience the semi-public oratory was erected object to the presence of other faithful, they may eject them, and the faithful in question must obey. On the other hand, if those in charge of the semi-public oratory freely admit other faithful, then those faithful, even though they have no strict right to enter the oratory, may do so licitly. It is clear, then, that the mere lack of the right to perform a certain act does not necessarily imply a prohibition to perform it. With this point established, the consideration of canon 2259, § 1, may be taken up..

Through the application of the principle *"odiosa sunt restringenda"* and also of the norm of canon 2219, namely, that relative to penalties the more benign interpretation is to be used, it seems safe to conclude that canon 2259, § 1, does not prohibit the *tolerati* from attending Mass, but merely deprives them of the right to attend. In other words the effect of the prescription of canon 2259, § 1, is this. A *toleratus* is deprived of his RIGHT to assist at Mass, and hence, may be expelled,[21] but if he is not expelled then he may licitly assist at the Holy Sacrifice.

The fact that canon 2259, § 1, uses the words *"caret iure"* certainly lends corroboration to this conclusion. It is hardly conceivable that the Church would use such a phrase if it intended to place a prohibition, especially in view of the controversy relative to the status of *tolerati* which existed prior to the promulgation of the Code. Furthermore the Code, in enumerating the other effects of excommunication, uses terminology that is clear and direct and which leaves no room for controversy, *e. g.*, *"prohibetur"* (can. 2261), *"non potest recipere"* (can. 2260, § 1), *"non fit particeps"* (can. 2262, § 1), *"nequit consequi"* (can. 2265, § 2), *"manet privatus"* (can. 2266), etc. In view of this fact, it seems hardly possible that the Church would use ambiguous terminology in the very first canon which treats of the effects of excommunication. Additional confirmation of this conclusion may be had by comparing canon 2259, § 1, with canon 2275, 1°. The latter canon states expressly that those who are un-

[21] Cf. Canon 2259, § 2.

der personal interdict cannot assist at the divine offices (*Personaliter interdict: Nequeunt divina officia . . . assistere*). These words evidently impose a prohibition. If canon 2259, § 1, also imposes a prohibition why did not the Church use similar unmistakable terminology? If it be argued that if the personally interdicted are forbidden to assist at the divine offices, *a fortiori* the excommunicated are, because excommunication is a more severe penalty than the interdict, a satisfactory answer is not wanting. The immediate purpose of the interdict is to deprive the delinquent of the use of certain sacred things enumerated in the canons, while the direct and immediate purpose of excommunication is to effect the separation of the delinquent from communion with his fellow-Christians. This can very satisfactorily explain why assistance at the divine offices may be forbidden to the personally interdicted, and not necessarily to the *tolerati,* even though excommunication considered in its total effect is a more severe penalty than the interdict.[22]

In the light of this reasoning, the writer feels justified in adopting the opinion that *tolerati,* by reason of canon 2259, § 1, are not prohibited from attending Mass but merely deprived of the right to do so, and that therefore they are bound to attend Mass on Sundays and Feastdays—an opinion supported by recognized authors.[23] In practice, however, in view of the doubt of law which exists concerning their obligation, the *tolerati* may be held as not bound by the precept.

(2) That the *vitandi,* before the adoption of the Code, were forbidden to attend the divine offices, has never been questioned. The Code in canon 2259, § 2, renews this prohibition by prescribing that if a *vitandus* assists passively at the divine offices, he must be expelled, and if he cannot be expelled, the divine office itself must be discontinued, provided that this can be done without grave incon-

[22] Conran, *The Interdict,* The Catholic University of America Canon Law Studies, n. 56 (Washington, D. C.: The Catholic University of America, 1930), p. 86.

[23] Blat, *Commentarium,* V (*De Delictis et Poenis*), n. 86; Vermeersch-Creusen, *Epitome,* III, n. 461; Ayrinhac, *Penal Legislation in the New Code of Canon Law* (New York: Benziger Bros., 1920), n. 115.

venience.[24] This prescription is certainly equivalent to a prohibition, and it would be futile to maintain otherwise, since all authors without exception interpret it as such. Hence it may be stated without hesitation that the *vitandi* are prohibited from assisting at Mass, as well as deprived of the right to do so.

The question arises, then, as to whether this admitted prohibition to attend Mass deletes the obligation of the *vitandi* to attend on the days when Mass is prescribed. One is inclined to answer this question with an emphatic "no," first on the principle that a delinquent should not benefit by his crime, and then on the implication of canon 87 which, while it states that a censure can impede rights, makes no similar statement with regard to duties. However this is not a question that can be answered by a single word. Authors hold divergent views regarding it and, in fact, quite generally maintain that the obligation is deleted by the prohibition. This makes it necessary to consider the question more at length.

The present writer is of the opinion that the prohibition to assist at divine offices, which is placed upon the *vitandi*, does not release them from the obligation of attending Mass on Sundays and Feastdays. In other words the obligation remains, and the censure merely constitutes an impediment which renders the delinquent unworthy of placing the prescribed act. Therefore the delinquent has an obligation to recede from his unworthiness in order that he might place the act which is prescribed.[25] This opinion, as supported by Michiels, seems sound enough. For there is no convincing reason why a prohibition to place a certain act necessarily deletes the obligation to place it. An example in point is the obligation to receive the Holy Eucharist during the Paschal Season. No one will deny that this obligation binds a man who is in mortal sin. Yet a man in mortal sin is prohibited from receiving Holy Communion because he is unworthy. The obligation is not deleted by this prohibition, but the basis of the prohibition, namely, the unworthiness, must be removed by sacramental absolution in order that he may fulfill his obligation.

[24] Canon 2259, § 2: *Si passive assistat toleratus, non est necesse ut expellatur; si vitandus, expellendus est, aut, si expelli nequeat, ab officio cessandum, dummodo id fieri possit sine gravi incommodo. . . .*

[25] Cf. Michiels, *Normae Generales,* I, 288, n. 1.

This example seems perfectly analogous to the case of an excommunicate who is under the obligation of hearing Mass. In each case there is an obligation to place a certain act. In each case there is also a prohibition to place that act, and the prohibition in each case is based on the same reason, namely, unworthiness to place it. Authors commonly admit that the obligation of receiving Paschal Communion is not deleted by the prohibition to receive the Eucharist in the case of those who are in mortal sin. They insist that the prohibition must be lifted by the removal of its cause, namely the unworthiness, through sacramental confession and absolution. Why, then, should not the same be true in the case of the excommunicate who is subject to the precept of hearing Mass? Why should the prohibition necessarily delete the obligation on the part of the *vitandi* to assist at Mass when it is prescribed? Yet many authors simply state that excommunicates are excused from the precept of hearing Mass because they are prohibited from assisting at the divine offices.[26] Other authors, perhaps recognizing that the prohibition does not necessarily delete the obligation, state that the prohibition contains a dispensation from the precept of hearing Mass.[27] That the Church, however, is willing to dispense from her laws those whom it is punishing with its most severe sanction remains to be proved. It is the writer's opinion, therefore, that in spite of the prohibition the obligation incumbent upon *vitandi* to hear Mass on Sundays and Feastdays still endures.

(3) The final question to be answered is this: What obligation have the *vitandi* to seek the removal of the censure of excommunication in order to render themselves worthy of assisting at Mass, and thereby enable themselves to fulfill the precept? If one holds, with the authors cited above, that the obligation of hearing Mass has ceased because of the prohibition, then the only logical answer to this question is that they have no obligation whatsoever to remove the censure in order to fulfill the precept. On the other hand, if one

[26] Maroto, *Institutiones Iuris Canonici,* I, n. 196, also footnote 3; Aertnys-Damen, *Theologia Moralis,* I, n. 530; Tanquerey, *Synopsis Theologiae Moralis,* II, n. 298; Lehmkuhl, *Theologia Moralis,* II, 638; Augustine, *Commentary,* VIII, 177.

[27] Cappello, *De Censuris,* n. 149; Chelodi-Dalpiaz, *Ius Poenale,* n. 37.

maintains, as the present writer maintains, that the obligation is not deleted by the prohibition, then it must be logically held that the *vitandi* have an obligation to remove the censure. It will be demonstrated in Chapter XII, Article V, b, of this study that one who is subject to the obligation of hearing Mass must take all the necessary means to fulfill that obligation, which includes the removal of impediments. It will also be pointed out in Article III of the same chapter that the obligation of attending Mass ceases when its discharge involves notable inconvenience. In the light of these two principles, therefore, it is the present writer's contention that the *vitandi* must seek the removal of the censure, which constitutes an impediment to their fulfillment of the precept, in order that they may hear Mass when it is prescribed, unless the removal would involve notable inconvenience. If they neglect to remove the censure when they can secure absolution without notable inconvenience, and foresee that they will miss Mass on a Sunday or Feastday because of their neglect, then they are guilty in cause of the violation of the precept and commit a mortal sin. Furthermore, if they foresee that, by neglecting to obtain the absolution which they could obtain without notable inconvenience, they will miss more than one Mass, then they are guilty in cause of as many mortal sins as there are prescribed Masses from the attendance at which they foresee they will be impeded. The sins are multiplied by reason of the plurality of objects.[28]

These conclusions do not enjoy the favor of many authors. St. Alphonsus inclines toward it when he states that more probably an excommunicate could not be excused from mortal sin if he could obtain absolution easily and neglected to do so, for every one is obliged to remove an impediment that can be removed without grave inconvenience in order to satisfy a grave precept. Aertnys-Damen adopt this opinion also.[29] It must be admitted, however, that the obligations of the *vitandi* as outlined above need not be urged in practice because the greater weight of authority adheres to the opinion that the *vitandi* are freed from their obligation of attending Mass and

[28] Cf. Aertnys-Damen, *Theologia Moralis,* I, n. 229.

[29] St. Alphonsus, *Theologia Moralis,* lib. III, n. 325; Aertnys-Damen, *Theologia Moralis,* I, n. 530. Also Ayrinhac, *Penal Legislation,* n. 115.

that they have no obligation to remove the censure in order to fulfill the precept, thereby giving rise to another doubt of law. The present writer, in investigating this problem at so great length, was not so presumptuous as to hope to overthrow by his argumentation the overwhelming weight of contrary authority, and thereby settle the question once and for all. It is his hope, however, that something has been contributed toward the ascertainment of objective truth relative to this problem.

It remains now to determine the obligation of those under interdict with regard to the precept of hearing Mass. In general, it may be said that the same conclusions which have been drawn concerning the obligation of excommunicates are equally applicable to the obligation of the interdicted. Certain distinctive features of the interdict, however, must be taken into account.

If the interdict is a local interdict, whether it be general or particular, the Code in canon 2271, 2°, provides that in each city or town at least one Mass may be celebrated. Therefore, on Sundays and Feastdays the faithful are obliged to assist at that Mass if they can do so without grave inconvenience, or if possible, to assist at Mass elsewhere.

If the interdict is personal, then according to canon 2275, 1°, those who are under it are forbidden to assist at Mass *(Personaliter interdicti nequeunt divina officia . . . assistere)*. Hence, their obligation is to be determined in the same manner as that of the *vitandi.*

If the interdict is *ab ingressu ecclesiae* (canon 2277) the persons who are under it are forbidden to assist at divine offices in a church. Since laws which state a penalty should, according to canon 19, receive a strict interpretation, the term *"ecclesia"* as used in canon 2277 must be interpreted strictly, that is, according to the definition of *"ecclesia"* as given in canon 1161. Hence, it does not include public or semi-public oratories.[80] Persons under such interdict are bound to fulfill their obligation in a public or semi-public oratory if they can do so without notable inconvenience.

Finally, if the interdict is inflicted as a vindictive penalty, the delinquent, if he be forbidden to assist at Mass, is excused from the

[80] Cappello, *De Censuris*, n. 472; Conran, *The Interdict*, p. 140.

precept until he can secure the proper dispensation without grave inconvenience.

To sum up the conclusions adopted by the present writer with regard to excommunicates and the interdicted: *tolerati* are bound to assist at Mass on Sundays and Feastdays; *vitandi* and those under personal interdict are bound to remove the censure in order to fulfill the precept when they can do so without notable inconvenience. These opinions have been adopted because, in the judgment of the writer, they enjoy greater intrinsic probability. In practice, however, the delinquents in question may be considered as free from the obligation of attending Mass by reason of a doubt of law. The conclusions drawn with regard to the obligations of the other interdicted need not be repeated.

Article II. Requisites on Part of Subject for Fulfillment of Precept

The first article of this chapter has determined the subject of the precept of hearing Mass, that is, who is bound by the obligation to hear Mass on Sundays and Feastdays. It is the purpose of the present article to determine those things which are demanded on the part of the subject in order that he may legitimately fulfill the obligation incumbent upon him.

The precept of hearing Mass is an ecclesiastical law the direct purpose of which is the sanctification of the individual through the public external worship of God. Therefore, in order that its purpose be attained, the subject must hear Mass *humano modo*. Since the subject is composed of body and will and intellect, each of these must be associated in some way with the hearing of Mass before it can truly be said to be heard in a human manner. Just what demands the precept makes regarding each of these elements will be investigated here.

(a) Moral Bodily Presence

On the part of the body there is required a moral presence. This is not to be confused with a moral personal presence, which could be effected through representation or by the use of a proxy, and which would not suffice for the fulfillment of the precept. In general the subject may be said to have moral bodily presence when he himself assists at Mass in union with the celebrant either directly or indirectly. He is in union with the celebrant directly if he can actually see the celebrant or hear his voice; he is in union with the celebrant indirectly if, unable to see or hear the celebrant himself, he can follow the progress of the sacrifice through the actions of his fellow worshipers, and is at the same time, according to the common estimation of men, a member of that multitude or group which is assisting at the Mass. That this moral bodily presence is required and is sufficient for the fulfillment of the precept is the common teaching of authors.[31]

In applying this norm, authors agree in general on the following conclusions.

The following have the required moral bodily presence:

(1) Those who are in the church proper, even though they be behind the altar or behind a pillar, or at a great distance from the celebrant. For these, even if they cannot see or hear the celebrant, can follow the progress of the Mass through the external actions of the congregation or by noting the ringing of the bell.

(2) Those who are in the choir or sacristy, or in some room or recess joined to the church, so long as they can directly or indirectly unite themselves with the celebrant. If, however, they are cut off from the church in such a manner that they cannot follow the progress of the Mass at all, either directly or indirectly, they cannot fulfill the precept.

(3) Those who are even outside of the church at any distance whatsoever, so long as they are actually united with the multitude that is present at the Mass. Some authors propose the norm that if they are separated from the crowd by a distance of thirty paces, they cannot be considered as one of the multitude. However, a better norm would be the common estimation of men as to whether

[31] St. Alphonsus, *Theologia Moralis*, lib. III, n. 312; Coronata, *De Locis et Temporibus Sacris*, n. 291; Gasparri, *De Sanctissima Eucharistia*, II, n. 953; Vermeersch, *Theologia Moralis*, III, n. 858; Tanquerey, *Synopsis Theologiae Moralis*, II, n. 1008; Merkelbach, *Summa Theologiae Moralis*, II, n. 701; Iorio, *Theologia Moralis*, II, n. 127; Aertnys-Damen, *Theologia Moralis*, I, n. 523; Lehmkuhl, *Theologia Moralis*, I, n. 715; and others.

or not they are morally united with and form part of the assisting multitude.

(4) Those in a nearby house who through a window can follow the motions of the celebrant or the congregation. It is impossible to determine exactly how near to the church the house must be. Once again the common estimation of men must be taken into account to determine whether persons assisting at Mass in that manner are or are not morally present.

It is evident that those who hear Mass over the radio or assist at it by observing the priest or the congregation through a telescope from a great distance, have not the required moral bodily presence and consequently do not fulfill the obligation.

(b) Intention of Hearing Mass

On the part of the will there is required the intention of hearing Mass. This intention is necessary because the Church prescribes the hearing of Mass as a religious act, and since the mere bodily presence of the subject at the Sacrifice is in itself indifferent, it must be determined as a religious act by the intention of hearing Mass.[32] Furthermore, it follows from the principle that, to satisfy an affirmative law, the placing of the prescribed act with the intention of doing that which the law commands is both requisite and sufficient.[33]

This required intention need not be actual, that is, made by the will actually at the time Mass is heard. It suffices that it be virtual, that is, elicited beforehand but enduring in such a way that it influences the act of hearing Mass, even though it may not be adverted to at the time the act is placed.

Nor need this intention be explicit, so that the person intends precisely to hear Mass. It suffices that it be implicit, that is, contained in some way in a more general intention, such as the intention of worshipping God, or of offering sacrifice, or of doing that which the rest of the faithful are doing.[34]

[32] Merkelbach, *Summa Theologiae Moralis,* II, n. 702.

[33] St. Alphonsus, *Theologia Moralis,* lib. I, n. 163; Aertnys-Damen, *Theologia Moralis,* I, n. 167; Marc-Gestermann, *Institutiones,* I, n. 211; Noldin-Schmitt, *De Principiis,* n. 171.

[34] Marc-Gestermann, *Institutiones,* I, n. 674; Merkelbach, *Summa,* II, n. 702.

Since the intention of hearing Mass as explained above is necessary for the fulfillment of the precept, it is evident that one who is present at Mass without such an intention, or *a fortiori,* one who makes a positive intention of not hearing Mass, does not fulfill his obligation.

It is very important to distinguish the intention of hearing Mass from the intention of fulfilling the precept. There is no obligation whatsoever on the part of the person to intend to fulfill the precept. The precept does not bind to formal obedience, that is, that the act be placed because it is prescribed, but only to material obedience, that is, that the act which is prescribed be placed. Therefore, if a person simply intends to hear Mass, without adverting to the fact that it is prescribed, or even if he make a positive intention of not fulfilling the precept, he places the act prescribed and therefore fulfills his obligation.[85]

(c) External Attention

On the part of the intellect there is certainly required external attention, and more probably also some internal attention.

External attention implies the avoidance of all those external actions which are incompatible with the hearing of Mass as a human and religious act. All authors admit that at least this is necessary for the fulfillment of the precept. Incompatible external actions may be defined as those which so occupy the mind of the subject as to completely distract him from the Sacrifice which is taking place.[86]

The following acts would be incompatible with the hearing of Mass as a human and religious act, and therefore would impede the required external attention:

(1) To assist at Mass in a state of complete intoxication; to sleep soundly throughout a notable portion of the Mass.

(2) To engage in serious conversation during a notable part of the Mass; to read profane books which require intense concentration, or even spiritual books for the exclusive sake of erudition, or curiosity, or information.

[85] St. Alphonsus, *Theologia Moralis,* I, n. 163; et omnes.

[86] Gasparri, *De Sanctissima Eucharistia,* n. 954.

(3) To write letters, or compose them; to examine intently the statues or pictures or decorations in the church; to concentrate intently on the music or singing; to spend a notable portion of the Mass in examining the clothing of others.

Such actions which completely distract the attention of the subject from the Mass are equivalent to the omission of the parts during which they are performed. It follows then, that the same norms which determine the obligation to supply omitted parts are to be applied in those cases where external attention has been impeded.[37]

The following actions are not considered fully incompatible with the hearing of Mass, and therefore do not impede the fulfillment of the precept:

(1) To assist at Mass in a state of slight intoxication; to sleep lightly and intermittently throughout the Mass.

(2) To engage in trivial and interrupted conversation; to read spiritual books for the sake of devotion; to recite the Breviary, or to say the penance received in Confession; to examine one's conscience.

(3) To serve at Mass, even though it be necessary to leave the sanctuary for short intervals; to sing in the choir; to play the organ or to ring the bells, so long as one attends in some way to the sacrifice being offered; to take up the collection, or to act as usher.

Most of the authors agree on the incompatible and compatible acts as listed above.[38]

(d) Confession

Whether the act of going to Confession is incompatible or compatible with the necessary external intention is a matter of dispute among authors. Some authors maintain that it does not impede the fulfillment of the precept as long as the penitent pays some atten-

[37] Cf. Chapter IX, Article III.

[38] St. Alphonsus, *Theologia Moralis,* lib. III, nn. 316-317; Aertnys-Damen, *Theologia Moralis,* I, n. 526; Gasparri, *De Sanctissima Eucharistia,* n. 954; Vermeersch, *Theologia Moralis,* III, n. 858; Coronata, *De Locis et Temporibus Sacris,* n. 291; Tanquerey, *Synopsis Theologiae Moralis,* II, nn. 1013-1014; Iorio, *Theologia Moralis,* II, nn. 132-133; Merkelbach, *Summa,* II, n. 702; Marc-Gestermann, *Institutiones,* I, n. 676.

tion to the Mass at the same time. They claim that through the pious act of confession God is sufficiently honored, since a confession made to a priest is the same as if it were made to Christ. St. Alphonsus once admitted the probability of this opinion, but later, in view of the common teaching to the contrary, rejected it as improbable.[39]

The common opinion, and the more probable one, is that the act of Confession is incompatible with the hearing of Mass because it impedes the necessary external attention, unless it is short and does not require intense concentration. For the penitent, even though he is present at the Mass, is there not as one offering sacrifice, but as an offender seeking absolution. Furthermore, Confession is an act, which of its nature demands concentration on the part of the one confessing, and therefore truly impedes the required external attention to the Mass. Some authors make an exception in regard to those who would be unable to go to Confession otherwise, and would have to remain for a notable period of time in mortal sin.[40] To the present writer it seems that in this case the necessity of confessing would constitute an excusing cause and release the penitent from the obligation of fulfilling the precept.

(e) Internal Attention

The question whether internal attention is required for the fulfillment of the precept offers some difficulty. By internal attention is meant the application of the mind to either the words and actions of the priest, as sacred things, or to the sacrifice itself, or to the Passion and Death of Christ, or to God through prayers or meditation or pious affections.[41]

While authors dispute in theory on this question, the practical conclusions they offer are quite similar. At any event, even those

[39] St. Alphonsus, *Theologia Moralis*, lib. III, n. 314.

[40] St. Alphonsus, *loc. cit.*; Tanquerey, *Synopsis Theologiae Moralis*, II, n. 1014; Marc-Gestermann, *Institutiones*, I, n. 676; Coronata, *De Locis et Temporibus Sacris*, n. 291; Gasparri, *De Sanctissima Eucharistia*, II, n. 954; Aertnys-Damen, *Theologia Moralis*, I, n. 527.

[41] Aertnys-Damen, *Theologia Moralis*, I, n. 524.

authors who in theory maintain that internal attention is necessary for the fulfillment of the precept, nevertheless admit that there is a doubt of law on the matter, and concede that the law does not bind. On the other hand, the authors who claim that internal attention is not necessary, hold that the precept is not fulfilled if a person indulges in distractions which are of such a nature that they completely impede attention to what is taking place.

As a practical norm the following may be offered: If a person intends to hear Mass, and abstains from all actions which are incompatible with that intention, he fulfills the precept.[42]

[42] Gasparri, Aertnys-Damen, and all others cited above.

CHAPTER XI

REQUIRED PLACE FOR THE FULFILLMENT OF THE PRECEPT

The matter about to be considered, namely, the place required for the fulfillment of the precept of hearing Mass, could have been appropriately included under the chapter devoted to the subject of the precept, since it is he who must be in the required place. In consideration, however, of the important fact that the hearing of Mass in one of certain determined places is a necessary condition for the fulfillment of the precept, and in view also of the fact that certain problems in connection with it demand rather lengthy discussion, it has seemed preferable to devote a separate chapter to the investigation of this question.

Article I. Ordinary Places Where Precept of Hearing Mass Can Be Fulfilled

Canon 1249: Legi de audiendo Sacro satisfacit qui Missae adest quocunque catholico ritu celebretur, sub dio aut in quacunque ecclesia vel oratorio publico aut semi-publico et in privatis coemeteriorum aediculis de quibus in can. 1190, non vero in aliis oratoriis privatis, nisi hoc privilegium a Sede Apostolica concessum fuerit.

(a) Fulfillment of Precept in a Different Rite

Canon 1249 states expressly that the precept of hearing Mass may be fulfilled by the attendance at Mass celebrated in any Catholic rite whatsoever. This is merely a repetition of the old law, and needs no explanation. The only doubt which may arise in connection with this is whether one would fulfill the precept if he were to hear Mass celebrated in a Catholic rite by a validly ordained priest of an heretical or schismatic sect. Though the attendance at such a

Mass is in itself gravely prohibited, and though one would commit a mortal sin by attending it, it seems probable nevertheless that the precept would be fulfilled.[1]

(b) Attendance at Parish Church No Longer Obligatory

Canon 1249 continues by enumerating the ordinary places where the precept of hearing Mass can be fulfilled, namely, in the open air, in any church or in any public or semi-public oratory, and in private cemetery chapels as described in canon 1190. These places will now be considered in order. In view of the fact, however, that the interpretation of the phrase *"sub dio"* is the object of controversy among authors, its consideration will be postponed and treated in a special article.

By the term "church" is meant a sacred edifice dedicated to divine worship, especially with a view to enabling all the faithful to practice public worship.[2] Since the Code makes no distinction, it follows that the precept can be fulfilled in any church, whether it be secular or religious, parochial or non-parochial. The obligation to attend Mass at the parish church is no longer in effect, because it has been abrogated not only by custom but also by subsequent decrees of popes, and this abrogation has been confirmed by the Code.[3] Ordinaries cannot prescribe the fulfilling of the precept of hearing Mass by attendance at the parish church, because such a prescription would be contrary to the common law. In particular instances ordinaries may be justified in making certain regulations in order to correct abuses which have arisen as a direct result of the utter neglect of the parish church on the part of a great number of parishioners. In no case, however, would such regulations have the effect that one who acted contrary to them would not fulfill the precept of hearing Mass. He would perhaps sin by disobedience in attending Mass on Sundays and Feastdays regularly in churches and

[1] Gasparri, *De Sanctissima Eucharistia,* n. 961; Vermeersch, *Theologia Moralis,* III, n. 859; Vermeersch-Creusen, *Epitome,* II, n. 563.

[2] Canon 1161. Translation of Woywod, *Practical Commentary,* n. 1198.

[3] Cf. Chapter V, Art. II.

oratories other than that of his own parish, but he would nevertheless always fulfill the precept of hearing Mass.[4]

(c) Public Oratories and Other Ordinary Places

A public oratory is an oratory which is erected mainly for the convenience of a body of men, or even of private individuals but in such a manner that all the faithful have a legitimately established right to enter the oratory, at least at the time of divine services.[5] It differs from a church in so far as it is intended primarily for the convenience of a certain group of persons rather than that of all the faithful. It is important to note, however, that all the faithful nevertheless have a strict right to frequent it at least at the time of divine services. Another difference is that, whereas the church is intended primarily for public worship, the oratory is intended rather for private devotion.[6]

A semi-public oratory is one which is erected for the convenience of a certain community or group of the faithful who assemble there, but the rest of the faithful are not free to enter it.[7] The difference between a public and a semi-public oratory consists chiefly in the matter of the right of all the faithful to frequent it. The faithful have a right to frequent public oratories, but they have no such right to frequent semi-public oratories. Therefore it is entirely within the power of the community or group in whose favor the semi-public oratory has been erected to refuse admission to others of the faithful who wish to enter it.

The oratories connected with religious houses are generally semi-

[4] Benedictus XIV, *De Synodo Dioecesana,* lib. XI, cap. 14, n. 8; St. Alphonsus, *Theologia Moralis,* lib. III, n. 322; Gasparri, *De Sanctissima Eucharistia,* n. 962; Iorio, *Theologia Moralis,* II, n. 135; Coronata, *De Locis et Temporibus Sacris,* n. 290; Bastnagel, "Assisting at Mass in the Parish Church," *ER,* CIV (1941), 463-467; Editor, "Sunday Mass and the Parish Church," *ER,* XCVIII (1938), 459-465.

[5] Canon 1188, § 2, 1°.

[6] Feldhaus, *Oratories,* p. 68.

[7] Canon 1188, § 2, 2°.

public as are also the oratories erected in educational institutions, hospitals, prisons, barracks, etc.[8]

By the cemetery chapels mentioned in canon 1249 are meant those which are erected by families or private individuals for their own sepulture. They are private oratories, as is evident from canon 1190, which treats of them, even though by reason of the fact that they are erected in a public place, namely, in a cemetery, they are not domestic oratories.

Such chapels, though quite numerous in Europe, are extremely rare in this country. The chapels usually erected in our cemeteries are not private oratories, but public oratories, since they are erected and intended as a general rule, not for a single individual or family, but for all the faithful who may wish to visit them. Such chapels are erected either directly by the local ordinary, or by the municipal authorities or cemetery corporation with the permission of the local ordinary, and therefore are public oratories in the strict sense of the term as defined by canon 1188, § 2, 1°. They must be distinguished, consequently, from the private cemetery chapels described in canon 1190. This distinction is of little importance to this study, however, since either type of oratory or chapel suffices as a legitimate place in which the precept of hearing Mass can be fulfilled.[9]

One who hears Mass in any of the places described above, namely, in a church, in a public or semi-public oratory, or in a cemetery chapel, fulfills his obligation.

(d) Private Oratories

The only place expressly excluded by canon 1249, and in which the precept of hearing Mass certainly cannot be fulfilled, is the private oratory. A private oratory is one which is erected in a private house for the convenience of some family or individual.[10] Since such oratories are usually erected in private homes and are destined exclusively for private use, they are known also as domestic oratories.

It is evident that the faithful at large have no right to frequent

[8] Canon 1192, § 4; S. R. C., decr. 23 ian. 1899—*Fontes,* 6288.

[9] Feldhaus, *Oratories,* p. 77.

[10] Canon 1188, § 2, 3°.

such oratories, since they have no right to frequent even semi-public oratories. The term "*familiae*" as used in the canon is to be understood in its natural and usual meaning, and therefore is not to be referred to corporations or moral persons whose physical members are sometimes referred to collectively as a "family." Hence, oratories erected in religious houses are not private oratories, but, as stated above, semi-public oratories.

According to canon 1249 the precept of hearing Mass cannot be fulfilled in a private oratory, except by those to whom this privilege has been conceded by the Holy See. In order to determine whether or not a particular person is so privileged, the indult which grants the right to possess and use a private oratory must be consulted. As a general rule, the indults grant the privilege of fulfilling the precept not only to those who are expressly named in the indult, but also to their relatives by consanguinity or affinity to the fourth degree inclusive, provided that they live in the house as members of the family. Furthermore the privilege is usually extended also to the noble guests of the persons to whom the indult is granted, as well as to those servants whose presence is necessary for the convenience of the privileged persons or for the service of the celebrant.[11] If persons other than those enumerated above attend Mass in a private oratory, they do not fulfill the precept of hearing Mass.

Certain exceptions to this prescription of canon 1249 may be indicated. The private oratories which cardinals and bishops, whether residential or titular, enjoy by reason of canons 239, § 1, 7°, and 349, § 1, though in the strict sense they are private oratories, nevertheless enjoy all the rights and privileges of semi-public oratories.[12] Therefore, in accordance with canon 1249, any one who hears Mass in such oratories may fulfill the precept.

Vicars and prefects apostolic, if they are bishops, naturally come under the privilege just described. If they are not bishops, however, they have all the privileges of protonotaries apostolic *de numero participantium.*[13] Among the privileges which these protonotaries

[11] Feldhaus, *Oratories*, p. 129; Ayrinhac, *Administrative Legislation*, n. 90; Vermeersch-Creusen, *Epitome*, III, n. 502; Iorio, *Theologia Moralis*, II, n. 134.

[12] Canon 1189.

[13] Canon 308.

enjoy is that of a private oratory in which the precept of hearing Mass may be fulfilled by all the faithful. This privilege was granted by the *Motu Proprio "Inter Multiplices"* (1905) of Pius X, and was renewed explicitly by Pope Pius XI in his Constitution *"Ad incrementum decoris"* (1934).[14]

Finally, permanently constituted apostolic administrators by virtue of canon 315 enjoy the same rights as are enjoyed by residential bishops, and therefore may have private oratories which enjoy all the rights and privileges of semi-public oratories. Those who hear Mass in such oratories can fulfill the precept.

It is probable that the priest celebrating the Mass, as well as the server, fulfills his obligation even when the Mass is said in a private oratory or in other places outside of a church or oratory. This conclusion is drawn from a benign interpretation of canon 1249, which enumerates the places where the law of *hearing* Mass may be fulfilled. The priest and server do not merely *hear* Mass.[15]

With regard to the fulfillment of the precept on board ship a distinction must be made. If Mass is heard in a fixed chapel, or in a room which is the equivalent of a fixed chapel, then such a place is considered a public oratory, and the precept is fulfilled.[16] Even if such a ship is in port, anyone can fulfill his obligation by attending Mass in its fixed chapel, even if he boards the ship precisely and only for that purpose.[17]

If, however, the ship has no fixed chapel, and the priest celebrates Mass by reason of a merely personal privilege in a cabin or in some other place, the precept in all probability cannot be fulfilled.[18] It would seem, therefore, that a priest on board ship who enjoys the privilege of the portable altar would have no obligation to celebrate Mass on Sunday in such a place in order to accommodate the faith-

[14] Pius X, motu propr. *Inter Multiplices,* 21 febr. 1905, n. 2, 12—*Fontes,* 665; Pius XI, const. *Ad incrementum decoris,* 15 aug. 1934, n. 46—*AAS,* XXVI (1934), 507.

[15] Vermeersch-Creusen, *Epitome,* II, n. 502; Iorio, *Theologia Moralis,* II, n. 136.

[16] S. R. C., *Vicen.,* 4 mart. 1901, ad V—*Fontes,* 6309.

[17] S. R. C., *Vicen.,* 10 maii 1901—*Fontes,* 6312.

[18] Iorio, *Theologia Moralis,* II, n. 137.

ful. The faithful in such a case are excused from the precept of hearing Mass by reason of the impossibility of its fulfillment. However, in order to fulfill his own obligation, the priest would be obliged to say Mass.

If the Mass is celebrated on deck in the open air, those hearing it would certainly discharge their obligation. This is clear from canon 1249 which expressly includes *"sub dio"* as a legitimate place for the fulfillment of the precept.

Article II. *"Sub Dio"*

(a) Opinion That "Sub Dio" Means "Ubicumque"

In enumerating the places where the precept of hearing Mass can be legitimately fulfilled, canon 1249 includes *"sub dio."* The classical and proper meaning of this phrase is "in the open air." Certain authors, however, interpret it as meaning any place which is not strictly private, or any place where Mass is said by reason of the privilege of the portable altar, etc.[19] Their opinions lead logically to this: the precept of hearing Mass can be fulfilled in any place where Mass is celebrated except in a private oratory. Unfortunately, most of the authors who subscribe to this extraordinary meaning of the phrase advance no reasons to justify their doing so. The few authors who do give reasons for their opinion, offer arguments which are not entirely convincing.

Beste, cited above, simply states that Mass celebrated anywhere by reason of the portable altar is morally *"sub dio."* This gratuitous assumption is hardly an argument.

Coronata, also cited above, argues that canon 1249 contains one lone exception regarding the place where the precept can be fulfilled, and that exception refers, not to the privilege of the portable altar, but only to strictly private oratories. He then concludes that the precept can be fulfilled in any place where the privilege of the portable altar is used. He continues by saying that many authors under

[19] Coronata, *De Locis et Temporibus Sacris,* n. 290; DeMeester, *Compendium,* n. 1148, scholion 1; Iorio, *Theologia Moralis,* II, n. 135; Konings-Putzer, *Commentarium in Facultates Apostolicas* (4. ed. Neo-Eboraci: Benziger Fratres, 1897), n. 161; Beste, *Introductio in Codicem,* p. 607.

the old law taught that the precept of hearing Mass prescribed only the hearing of Mass without any determination of place, and that therefore it could be fulfilled in any place whatsoever. The Code, he says, determined the place by excluding only private oratories. Therefore he concludes that, under the present discipline, the precept can be fulfilled in any place whatsoever outside of churches, when Mass is celebrated by privilege of the portable altar, with the one exception of private oratories. He concedes that if the indult granting the privilege of the portable altar expressly states otherwise, it must be followed.

The arguments adduced by Coronata do not seem sufficiently strong to warrant his opinion. In the first place, it may be said that the Code in canon 1249 does exclude places other than private oratories, at least implicitly, by the very fact that it uses the phrase *"sub dio,"* whose proper meaning is "in the open air." If it be asked why the canon expressly excludes private oratories when they too have to be considered as implicitly excluded by the phrase *"sub dio,"* it may be answered that it does so to leave no doubt in the matter. For the canon states that the precept can be fulfilled in the private cemetery chapels described in canon 1190, and then immediately adds "not, however, in other private oratories." [20] This explicit exclusion of private oratories may well have been included in order to preclude any speculation on the part of authors as to whether the fulfillment of the precept might not be justified even in other private oratories which were not cemetery chapels. For it is very possible that, had not the phrase *"non vero in aliis oratoriis privatis"* been added, canonists and moralists might have argued that since the precept could be fulfilled in private cemetery chapels, then surely it could be fulfilled in private oratories. Whether or not authors would have resorted to such argumentation, the fact remains that by explicitly excluding private oratories, the canon does preclude any speculation on the matter.

Coronata's other argument, the appeal to the opinion of pre-

[20] Canon 1249: Legi de audiendo Sacro satisfacit qui Missae adest . . . in privatis coemeteriorum aediculis de quibus in can. 1190, non vero in aliis oratoriis privatis . . .

Code authors, seems equally unconvincing. The opinions of recognized pre-Code authors need be followed only when the Code has taken over the old law in its entirety, or in part.[21] It is not clear that canon 1249 adopted the old law. In fact, it is reasonably certain that it did not, because the old law did not employ the phrase *"sub dio,"* and pre-Code authors therefore did not base their conclusion that the precept could be fulfilled anywhere on an interpretation of that phrase. In order to draw the conclusion that canon 1249 changes the old law only in so far as it excludes private oratories, it would seem necessary first to determine precisely what is the content of canon 1249. Coronata, however, seems to take for granted that the explicit exclusion of private oratories is the only change introduced by the new law, and then uses that presumption as a basis for his argument that *"sub dio"* must necessarily mean "anywhere." This process, it seems to the writer, must be reversed. First, determine what the canon means by the phrase *"sub dio,"* and then, on the basis of that determination, decide whether the Code does or does not introduce a change from the old law. If it does, follow the interpretation of the canon; if it does not, follow the interpretation of pre-Code authors. It is the opinion of the present writer that the phrase *"sub dio"* as used in canon 1249 can mean only "in the open air" and that therefore the old law has been changed by the Code.

(b) Better Opinion That "Sub Dio" Means "in the Open Air"

Canon 18 states that ecclesiastical laws are to be understood according to the proper meaning of the words taken in their text and context. If the meaning of the words is clear, no interpretation is necessary. It is only when the meaning is doubtful or obscure, or when it admits of a wider or of a stricter interpretation, that one is justified in proceeding to the other norms of interpretation as given by canon 18.[22]

The classical, proper and only meanings of the phrase *"sub dio"* is

[21] Canon 6, 2°, 3°.

[22] Canon 18; DeMeester, *Compendium,* n. 271; Michiels, *Normae Generales,* I, 379.

"in the open air" or "under the open sky," etc. The meaning, therefore, is clear and there seems to be no justification for attributing to the phrase any other meaning. If the legislator intended to convey the idea that the precept of hearing Mass can be fulfilled in any place whatsoever, why did he use a classical phrase whose only and exclusive meaning is "in the open air"? Furthermore, if he intended to state that the Mass precept could be fulfilled everywhere outside of private oratories, why did he bother to enumerate churches, public oratories, semi-public oratories and private cemetery chapels, when all of these could have been included, with equal clarity, under the term *"ubicumque"* or some other synonymous word?

Konings-Putzer, in their commentary on the Apostolic Faculties granted to this country by the Sacred Congregation for the Propagation of the Faith, apparently interpret the phrase *"sub dio"* to mean *"in loco profano."* [23] However, in doing so, they may have been acting on the principle that the greater includes the less. Faculties granted to missionary countries by the Congregation for the Propagation generally employ the words *"etiam sub terra et sub dio, in loco tamen decenti,"* [24] thereby implying that the mere grant of the privilege of the portable altar does not always include the right to celebrate Mass in the open air or under the earth. Gasparri tesifies that when the Holy See granted the privilege of the portable altar, it usually added the words *"missam celebrari non posse, nisi in loco honesto et tuto."* And it is Gasparri's contention that when such words were included in the indult, then Mass could not be celebrated in the open air or on the sea, because such places were not safe because of the danger arising from the wind, etc.[25]

Therefore it is quite evident that the faculty of celebrating Mass in the open air was usually superadded to the ordinary faculty of celebrating Mass in other profane places outside of a church. It is not impossible that Konings-Putzer took that fact into consideration when they interpreted the phrase *"sub dio"* to signify *"in loco profano."* They may have simply deduced that if the Apostolic Facul-

[23] Konings-Putzer, *Commentarium in Facultates Apostolicas,* n. 161.

[24] Cf. Blat, *Commentarium,* lib. III, pars I, p. 718.

[25] Gasparri, *De Sanctissima Eucharistia,* n. 272.

ties gave the superadded faculty to celebrate in the open air, they also gave the ordinary faculty to celebrate in other profane places.

That the Holy See uses the words *"sub dio"* to signify "in the open air" is evident from documents which have been issued even since the Code. For example, in the Index of faculties issued by the Sacred Consistorial Congregation to *vicarii castrenses* and major chaplains of all nations which are in a state of war, the faculty is granted *"litandi Sacrum loco honesto atque decenti, etiam sub dio et in navi . . ."* [26] That the phrase *"sub dio"* as used in this faculty signifies "in the open air" is evident from the fact that the wording of the faculty continues *"quoties Missa litatur sub dio, ad impediendam fragmentorum SS.mae Eucharistiae dispersionem causa ventorum, ad hoc adhibito tentorio ad tria latera altaris descendente."*

In the same way, Pope Pius XI in granting certain privileges to pilgrims on their way to the Holy House of Loretto, included the privilege of celebrating Mass *"sub divo"* provided that the necessary safeguards were taken to prevent the sacred particles from being dispersed by the wind.[27]

In consideration of the fact, therefore, that the Holy See did and does use the phrase *"sub dio"* to signify "in the open air," it is hardly conceivable that it used it in the Code to signify "in any place whatsoever."

It is true that the Analytical Index of the Code, in indicating the places where the precept of hearing Mass can be fulfilled, contains the word *"ubivis."* This fact seems negligible, however, in the light of the arguments which have been adduced in favor of the contrary opinion. At any rate, it is not an authoritative or official source of interpretation.

Therefore the writer of the present study maintains that the phrase *"sub dio"* as used in canon 1249 means "in the open air," and that any more extensive interpretation of its meaning is unjustified. The only possible conclusion, then, is that any person who hears Mass outside of a church, public or semi-public oratory, private cemetery chapel, or private oratory, does not, by reason of

[26] S. C. C. *Index facultatum,* 8 dec. 1939—*AAS,* XXXI (1939), 710.

[27] Pius XI, litt. apost. *Romani Pontifices,* 6 aug. 1936—*AAS,* XXIX (1937), 50.

canon 1249, fulfill the precept, unless he attends a Mass celebrated in the open air. This opinion is supported by many authors.[28]

Article III. Extraordinary Places for Fulfillment of Precept

(a) Mass Outside of Churches and Oratories

In the conclusion of the preceding article it was stated that the precept of hearing Mass cannot be fulfilled in any other place outside of churches, etc., except in the open air. This conclusion was drawn solely from a consideration of canon 1249, which enumerates the ordinary places where the precept can be legitimately fulfilled. It is to be understood, therefore, in the sense that places other than the open air, which do not correspond to one of the places enumerated in canon 1249, such as parish halls, auditoriums and the like, are not ordinary places for the legitimate fulfillment of the precept. It is entirely possible that such places can, in extraordinary circumstances, serve for the fulfillment of the Sunday and Feastday obligation. It is the purpose of this article to determine under what circumstances they can.

Canon 822, § 4, states:

> Loci Ordinarius aut, si agatur de domo religionis exemptae, Superior maior, licentiam celebrandi extra ecclesiam et oratorium super petram sacram et decenti loco, nunquam autem in cubiculo, concedere potest iusta tantum ac rationabili de causa, in aliquo extraordinario casu et per modum actus.

This power granted to local ordinaries and major superiors of exempt religions, is substantially the same as the power enjoyed by local ordinaries before the Code, except that it is restricted to extraordinary cases.

The Council of Trent took away from bishops the faculty they had previously enjoyed of permitting the celebration of Mass *"pri-*

[28] Ayrinhac, *Administrative Legislation,* n. 91; Aertnys-Damen, *Theologia Moralis,* I, n. 528; Marc-Gestermann, *Institutiones,* I, n. 677; Woywod, *Practical Commentary,* n. 1275.

vatis in domibus" sive "omnino extra ecclesiam et ad divinum tantum cultum dedicata oratoria." [29] Authors, however, commonly interpreted this revocation by the Council of Trent as applying only to the power of permitting Mass to be celebrated outside of churches, etc., *perpetuo per modum habitus.* They based this mild interpretation on the fact that the Council used the words *"Neve patiantur* Episcopi . . . ," and argued that, had the Council intended to abolish totally the power of bishops in this regard, it would have used a more severe and unmistakable terminology. Therefore they commonly subscribed to the opinion that bishops, even after the Council of Trent, enjoyed the power of permitting Mass to be said outside of churches and oratories *per modum actus* in cases of grave necessity.[30]

Many responses of the Holy See corroborated this opinion of pre-Code authors by recognizing the power of bishops to permit Mass to be said outside of churches and oratories for a grave cause and *per modum actus.*[31] Therefore there can be little doubt that under the pre-Code discipline bishops had the power to permit the celebration of Mass outside of churches and oratories *per modum actus* in cases of grave necessity.

(b) Present Power of Bishops in This Regard

Some authors, interpreting canon 822, § 4, of the new Code, concluded that the old law was changed by the new inasmuch as the new law demanded only a just and reasonable cause to warrant the permission, whereas the old demanded a grave cause. This opinion has been rejected by the Holy See itself, for in a letter to the ordinaries of Italy, the Sacred Congregation of the Sacraments clearly asserted that canon 822, § 4, confirms the traditional discipline with regard to

[29] Conc. Trident., sess. XXII, *de observandis et evitandis in celebratione missae.*

[30] St. Alphonsus, *Theologia Moralis,* lib. VI, n. 359; Lehmkuhl, *Theologia Moralis,* II, 167; Many, *Praelectiones de Missa* (Paris: Letouzey et Ané, 1903), n. 5; Gasparri, *De Sanctissima Eucharistia,* n. 275; Wernz, *Ius Decretalium,* III, n. 457.

[31] S. C. de Prop. Fide, decr. 18 nov. 1765—*Fontes,* 4547; S. C. de Sacramentis, *Meliten.,* 22 mart. 1915, ad I—*Fontes,* 2110; *Romana et aliarum,* 23 dec. 1912, ad I—*Fontes,* 2107.

this matter.[32] The secretary of the same Congregation, in the annotations officially published in connection with a response of May 3, 1926, stated:

> . . . From this obligation (that of saying Mass in a church or oratory), according to the ancient practice there was but one excuse, namely, a *great* (c. 1, D. I, *de consecr.*) or *supreme necessity* (c. 11, D. I, *cit.*). . . .
>
> . . . Has the Code effected a change? Some think so, and seem to be influenced by the fact that the Code requires a *just and reasonable* cause; from which they conclude that the cause need not be a grave one.
>
> But if one considers that not only the reason for the permission must be just and reasonable, but besides that the permission must be given only by way of act, and only in an extraordinary case, it can reasonably be inferred that there is no change in this respect. For the gravity of the cause, or necessity, is to be taken in moral estimation; and since c. 822, § 4, requires not only that the cause be just and reasonable, but that the permission be granted by the ordinary only by way of act and in some extraordinary case, surely we have then a case of moral necessity. And therefore no change has been introduced in the old law and jurisprudence. (Translation of Bouscaren, *CLD*, I, 388.) [33]

There can be little doubt, then, that canon 822, § 4, at least as far as the cause necessary for the grant of permission is concerned, has taken over and confirmed the discipline as it existed before the Code.

Pre-Code authors in considering the cause required for the legitimate use of the faculty on the part of ordinaries, invariably included the necessity of the faithful to fulfill the precept of hearing Mass. In giving examples of such cases of necessity all agreed that the need of a great number of the faithful to fulfill the precept constituted the grave cause as required. Therefore they stated that the ordinary could give the permission, *e. g.*, when the church was destroyed; when it was too small to accommodate the faithful on a solemn feast; when because of pestilence Mass could not be said in

[32] S. C. de Sacramentis, litt. ad Rev.mos Ordinarios Italiae. 26 iul. 1924—*AAS,* XVI (1924), 370-371.

[33] S. C. de Sacramentis, *Romana et aliarum,* 3 maii 1926, *adnotationes,* ad 1—*AAS,* XVIII (1926), 389-390.

the church; when because of flood or earthquake, etc., the faithful could not safely go to church, etc.[34]

As a matter of fact, some authors were hesitant to admit that a grave necessity could exist unless it involved the obligation of the faithful to fulfill the precept. To quote Gasparri:

> Haec necessitas in genere verificatur quando ecclesia vel oratorium non adest, aut adiri non potest, vel non sine magno incommodo a fidelium multitudine quae proinde Missa cui assistere debet careret nisi haec extra ecclesiam aut oratorium celebraretur.[35]

Also:

> Porro in relatis necessitatis casibus Missae celebratio extra ecclesiam et oratorium publicum permitti non potest nisi diebus festis, cum in diebus ferialibus necessitas assistendi Missae non adsit.[36]

(c) Fulfillment of Precept When Mass Is Permitted Outside of Church

Since the necessity of fulfilling the precept on the part of a great number of the faithful was commonly recognized as constituting a grave necessity under the old law, and therefore warranted the grant of the permission for Mass to be said outside of churches and oratories, and since canon 822, § 4, merely confirms the old law as far as the required cause is concerned, it seems reasonable to conclude that a similar cause would justify local ordinaries and major superiors in exercising their power today. The only difficulty lies in the fact that the faithful cannot fulfill the precept of hearing Mass in places other than those enumerated in canon 1249, which places, as has been shown in the preceding article, do not include any place outside of churches and oratories except the open air. The solution to this difficulty is this: the power granted by canon 822, § 4, to local ordinaries and major superiors implicitly contains also the power to

[34] St. Alphonsus, *Theologia Moralis,* lib. VI, n. 356; Many, *De Missa,* n. 6; Gasparri, *De Sanctissima Eucharistia,* n. 276.

[35] Gasparri, *op. cit.*, n. 274.

[36] Gasparri, *op. cit.*, n. 278; Many, *op. cit.*, n. 6, 2°.

dispense from the required place for the fulfillment of the precept of hearing Mass.

The reasons which prompt this conclusion are these. It has been shown that ordinaries and major superiors under the new Code can grant the permission in question for the same reasons which justified ordinaries before the Code in granting it. Therefore they can grant the permission in order to enable a great number of the faithful to fulfill the precept of hearing Mass, which they could otherwise not do. If the faithful, by reason of whose necessity the permission was granted, could not fulfill the precept even when such permission was granted, due to the fact that the place where Mass was said was not a legitimate one for the discharge of the obligation, the power enjoyed by the local ordinary or major superior would be useless.

Canon 66, § 3, states that when a faculty is granted it includes all other powers which are necessary for its use.[37] For the use of the faculty granted in canon 822, § 4, the power of dispensing from the prescribed place for the fulfillment of the precept is necessary. Therefore, by virtue of canon 66, § 3, local ordinaries and major superiors can dispense from the required place. That the power of dispensing from the common law can be granted implicitly by the Code is evident from canon 81 which states:

> A generalibus Ecclesiae legibus Ordinarii infra Romanum Pontificem dispensare nequeunt . . . nisi haec potestas eisdem fuerit explicite vel *implicite* concessa. . . .

The objection may justly be raised here that the power granted to ordinaries by canon 822, § 4, is not a "faculty" as contemplated in canon 66, § 3, but rather ordinary power, and that therefore canon 66, § 3, does not apply. It is true that the power which bishops enjoy to allow Mass to be celebrated outside of churches and oratories is ordinary power. However, since there is no express provision of law with regard to special powers granted to an office by the Code (ordinary power), it seems safe to proceed according to the prescription of canon 20, which states: *Si certa de re desit expressum*

[37] Canon 66, § 3: Concessa facultas secumfert alias quoque potestates quae ad illius usum sunt necessariae; . . .

praescriptum legis . . . norma sumenda est . . . a legibus latis in similibus. The power granted to bishops as ordinary power in canon 822, § 4, corresponds to the similar, though more extensive, power usually granted to ordinaries in the Apostolic Faculties. Canon 66, § 3, is applicable to the Apostolic Faculties, and therefore, by reason of canon 20, would also seem to be applicable to the power as granted in canon 822, § 3.

Therefore, it is the conclusion of this study that when local ordinaries grant permission for Mass to be celebrated outside of churches or oratories in order to enable a great number of the faithful to fulfill the precept of hearing Mass, then that permission contains also a dispensation from the observance of the requisite place, with the result that at least all those faithful, whose necessity is the cause for the permission, can fulfill the precept in any place where the permitted Mass is celebrated.[88]

(d) "In an Extraordinary Case"

It remains now to determine under what conditions the local ordinary or the major superior of an exempt religious institute can grant such a permission. Canon 822, § 4, which grants them that faculty, also places the conditions necessary for its legitimate use. The permission can be granted only for a just and reasonable cause, in an extraordinary case, and *per modum actus,* but never for Mass to be celebrated in a bedroom. It has already been shown that the necessity of a large number of the faithful to fulfill the precept constitutes a sufficient cause for the lawful exercise of the faculty. Therefore, the interpretation of the phrases "*in aliquo casu extraordinario*" and "*per modum actus*" alone remains to be considered.

Preparatory to considering this double question, it may be said, first of all, that the power granted by canon 822, § 4, is ordinary power, and may be delegated totally or in part, in accordance with canon 199, § 1.[89] Secondly, since canon 822, § 4, contains an excep-

[88] Cf. Bouscaren, "De Missa ex licentia Ordinarii celebrata," *Periodica de Re Morali Canonica Liturgica* (Bruges, 1905—), XXVIII (1939), 52-61; Prümmer, *Manuale Theologiae Moralis,* II, 395.

[89] S. C. de Sacramentis, resp. 29 iul. 1927, *adnotationes—AAS,* XX (1928), 79.

tion from the law as stated in canon 822, § 1, which prescribes that Mass must be celebrated in a church or oratory, it must, by reason of canon 19, be interpreted strictly.[40] The Holy See has on a number of occasions corroborated this statement.[41]

It is difficult to determine precisely what canon 822, § 4, intends by the words "in an extraordinary case." A "case," as will be shown in Chapter XIII, Article II, of this study, is determined as such by the cause which warrants the use of the faculty. The case endures as long as the cause which determines it endures. If the cause will endure permanently or indefinitely, then the case determined by it will endure in the same way; if the cause is transient, then the case will also be transient. To illustrate: a certain cause exists in a parish by reason of which a great number of the faithful are unable to hear Mass on Sunday or on a Feastday, *e. g.*, the church is too small to accommodate all the parishioners. This cause determines the case, because it is in view of this cause that the faculty of the local ordinary to permit Mass outside of the church can be used. If the cause will endure permanently, *e. g.*, a new church will never be built, then the case will endure permanently. If the cause, however, is only transient, *e. g.*, a new church is under way, then the case is transient.

Canon 822, § 4, demands an "extraordinary case." It is in determining just what is meant by "extraordinary" that the real difficulty lies. If a certain "case" is common in a certain territory, then it certainly cannot be considered as extraordinary in relation to that territory. For example, if it is a common situation in the United States that parish churches cannot accommodate all the parishioners for Sunday Mass, then an individual "case" of that kind cannot be considered extraordinary in relation to the United States. However, cases that are ordinary relatively to a certain territory by reason of the fact that such cases are common there, can be extraordinary in relation to other territories where such cases are rare. For example, the case given in the example above, which is only an ordinary case in relation to the United States, can be an extraordinary case if it is

[40] Michiels, *Normae Generales,* I, 450.

[41] P. C. I., 16 oct. 1919, ad XII—*AAS,* XI (1919), 478; S. C. de Sacramentis, decr. 3 maii 1926—*AAS,* XVIII (1926), 388-391; litt. ad Ordinarios Italiae, 26 iul. 1924—*AAS,* XVI (1924), 370.

viewed in relation to the entire Church, because cases of that kind are not common throughout the whole Christian world.

The important question to be answered, then, in order to determine the meaning of "extraordinary case" as used in the canon, is this: Must the case be extraordinary relatively to the diocese or country of the one who grants the permission, or must it be extraordinary only in relation to the entire Christian world?

If a bishop in an enactment of a diocesan synod gave a faculty which could be exercised only in an extraordinary case, then it would seem that the case would have to be extraordinary in relation to the diocese. Similarly, if a plenary council issued a similar faculty the case most probably would have to be extraordinary in relation to the country in which the plenary council was held. Since, however, the Code legislates for the universal Church, it seems reasonable to conclude that the "extraordinary case" which it demands in canon 822, § 4, need be extraordinary only in relation to the universal Church.

The import of this conclusion is obvious. For in the United States many situations exist which are peculiar to it, and which do not exist in most of the other parts of the Christian world. While these "cases" may be considered ordinary cases in the United States, they are nevertheless extraordinary cases in relation to the universal Church. To enumerate some of these cases: parishes in which, due to the rapid growth of the membership, the parish church cannot accommodate all the parishioners for Sunday Mass; country "missions" where the people are too poor to erect a church and consequently have none; non-sectarian institutions in which, due to civil law or because of the opposition of authorities, an oratory or chapel cannot be erected, etc. These cases may be common and therefore ordinary in this country; in relation to the universal Church, however, they can truly be considered extraordinary.

It is the opinion of the present writer that the cases considered above warrant the exercise of the faculty enjoyed by local ordinaries and major superiors by reason of canon 822, § 4. To the writer's knowledge, no author has explicitly considered this particular question. Most of the authors, in giving examples of the "extraordinary case" limit themselves to examples which can be truly called extraordinary even in relation to the particular territory. The following examples are typical: the emergency arising because of a convention of Boy Scouts, or because of a rally of Catholic Action groups, or because of the destruction of the parish church; the situation prevalent in army camps, etc.[42] However, none of these authors deny that the faculty can be exercised in the cases considered at length above. Hence it is the opinion of the writer that the faculty can legitimately be exercised in such cases.

(e) "Per Modum Actus"

Even more difficulty is encountered in the attempt to determine exactly what is meant by the phrase *"per modum actus."* As has already been stated in Chapter VIII, Article III of this study, authors offer a wide variety of interpretations for this phrase. In commenting on the phrase as used in this very connection with the power of ordinaries to permit Mass outside of churches, authors manifest a vast difference in opinion as to what *"per modum actus"* signifies. For example Lehmkuhl interprets it to mean *"non habitualiter, sed pro singulis vicibus seu una alterave vice."* [43] Sabetti-Barrett, on the other hand, state as follows: *"Per modum actus" non necessario significat semel tantum sed excludit habitualiter. Si aliqua transitoria ratio habetur, ea durante, concedi potest facultas.*

All authors without exception admit that *"per modum actus"* is opposed to *"per modum habitus."* But unfortunately this phrase is also very difficult to interpret.

It is certain that the ordinary or major superior cannot grant permission for Mass to be celebrated perpetually outside of a church or oratory in any given case. It is equally certain that he cannot by one and the same act give permission for Mass to be said outside of churches, etc., in a case which will endure for an extended period of time, for there can be little doubt that such a permission would be granted *"per modum habitus."*

[42] Bouscaren, "De Missa ex licentia Ordinarii celebrata," *Periodica,* XXVIII (1939), 58; Vermeersch-Creusen, *Epitome,* II, n. 100; Noldin-Schmitt, *De Sacramentis,* n. 201, 4; Cappello, *De Sacramentis,* I, n. 751.

[43] *Theologia Moralis,* II, 167.

Furthermore, it does not seem probable that he can give permission for Mass to be said *"durante causa"* if the cause and the case determined by it will endure for more than a few weeks, because this would certainly seem to be a distortion of the idea of the phrase *"per modum actus."* It is true that some authors claim that the permission to celebrate "often" or to celebrate eight or ten times would still come under the concept of *"per modum actus,"* [44] but even this seems to be stretching the phrase a bit too far.

It is the opinion of the author that the phrase *"per modum actus"* means that the concession can be made for only one act, and that its meaning in relation to canon 822, § 4, is that the permission can be granted for one celebration of Mass outside of a church or oratory. This opinion is drawn in consideration of the fact that canon 822, § 4, must be interpreted strictly. The strict interpretation of *"per modum actus"* would seem to be that it is limited to one Mass. This statement is corroborated by an observation made in the annotations officially published in connection with a response of the Sacred Congregation of the Sacraments. To establish the point that the power of bishops relative to allowing the celebration of Mass outside of churches and oratories should be restricted, the Secretary of the aforesaid Congregation makes use of the following argument: To allow the bishop to grant permission for a number of Masses does not seem to be reconcilable with canon 1194. Canon 1194 declares: "In other domestic oratories the ordinary of the place can permit the celebration of only one Mass, by way of act, for a just and reasonable cause, in some extraordinary case." Would it not certainly argue a want of harmony in the law, if in oratories only one Mass could be permitted by the ordinary, while outside of oratories, and hence outside of sacred places altogether, the celebration of more than one Mass were permitted? [45] This argument certainly lends considerable weight to the contention that the phrase *"per modum actus"* as used in canon 822, § 4, signifies strictly that the ordinary can give permission for only one Mass. In view of the fact, however, that this

[44] Cappello, *De Sacramentis,* I, n. 751; Blat, *Commentarium,* lib. III, pars I, p. 146; Cocchi, *Commentarium,* V, n. 32.

[45] S. C. de Sacramentis, resp. 3 maii 1926, *adnotationes—AAS,* XVIII (1936), 391.

interpretation is given only rarely by authors,[46] it seems safe in practice to extend the strict interpretation so as to include the giving of permission for one or the other time, or for a few times, as some authors hold.[47]

The above-cited response of the Sacred Congregation countenances this opinion, inasmuch as it states that the ordinary, on the occasion of the death of certain distinguished persons, can permit one or two Masses in the funeral chamber, but not more than three.

If the "case" is one which will endure for a short time, there seems to be no compelling reason why the local ordinary cannot give permission for Mass to be celebrated outside of a church for the duration of the cause, not indeed by giving a blanket permission by one act, but by renewing the permission each individual time it is required, or at least every two or three weeks. The inconvenience attendant upon the frequent renewal of permission could be very easily eliminated by the delegation of the ordinary's power to the pastor or priest of the parish in which the "case" exists.

If, however, the "case" is of such a nature that it will endure permanently, or for an extended period of time, it seems necessary that the ordinary apply to the Holy See for a special indult, either for the particular case, or for all cases of the same nature. While the recourse to the Holy See is being made, he could exercise his faculty as indicated above.[48]

The reason prompting the conclusion just given is that, if the local ordinary were to give permission even *"per modum actus"* for cases that of their nature will endure permanently, or for a long time, he would seem not to be acting according to the mind of the Church, for the Church manifestly does not favor the unlimited exercise of this faculty.[49]

If conditions are such that permanent or long-enduring cases of

[46] Augustine, *Commentary,* IV, 173.

[47] Lehmkuhl, *Theologia Moralis,* II, 167; Vermeersch-Creusen, *Epitome,* II, n. 552.

[48] Cappello, *De Sacramentis,* I, n. 750.

[49] P. C. I., 16 oct. 1919, ad XII—*AAS,* XI (1919), 478; S. C. de Sacramentis, decr. 3 maii 1926—*AAS,* XVIII (1926), 388-391; 26 iul. 1924—*AAS,* XVI (1924), 370.

this kind are quite common, as they seem to be in many dioceses of this country, the resultant situation can be very well compared to the situation which exists in missionary countries, for which the Holy See through the Sacred Congregation for the Propagation of the Faith is accustomed to give to ordinaries a special faculty by which they can allow missionaries and priests to say Mass outside of churches and oratories. If the bishops of those countries could solve the difficulty simply by giving the permissions "*per modum actus,*" or by delegating the priests themselves with the power to give the required permission on every occasion when it is necessary, then the Apostolic Faculties in this particular regard would seem to be unnecessary.

In the Apostolic Faculties granted to the ordinaries of Latin America by Pope Pius XI in 1929, the faculty of permitting priests the use of the portable altar for the benefit of the faithful in cases wherein a church or oratory was lacking, or too far distant, was granted to the said ordinaries. In the introduction to these faculties Pope Pius stated that, due to the promulgation of the Code of Canon Law and the altered conditions of the times, some changes were to be desired in the tenor of the concession of faculties as formerly made, and that therefore He was giving a new schema of privileges. While this does not necessarily mean that the faculties, as given before, were changed to conform to the Code, it does indicate that the new schema of faculties was drawn up with the New Code in view. And therefore, it seems reasonable to expect that the faculties as granted by Pope Pius XI in 1929 granted powers to ordinaries over and above those which they already enjoyed by reason of the Code. If, by virtue of canon 822, § 4, ordinaries are empowered to permit Mass to be celebrated outside of churches and oratories in cases which are permanent or long-enduring, then the faculty mentioned above seems superfluous.[50] For this reason it is the opinion of the present writer that when the ordinary foresees that a case will endure permanently or even for a long period of time, he should apply to the Holy See for a special indult to allow Mass to be said outside of a church or oratory, and not attempt to provide for the case by virtue of canon 822, § 4.

[50] Pius XI, *litterae apostolicae,* 30 apr. 1929, n. 8—*AAS,* XXI (1929), 556.

CHAPTER XII

EXCUSING CAUSES RELATIVE TO THE PRECEPT OF HEARING MASS

WITH relation to every ecclesiastical law there exist certain excusing causes. By the term "excusing cause" as used in this chapter is meant a cause which by itself is of sufficient gravity to excuse one who is subject to a law from the obligation of fulfilling it. Therefore in its concept is not to be included exemption, which connotes that a person is not subject to the law, nor dispensation, which is a relaxation of the law by a competent superior in favor of a subject for a cause which need not be grave enough to excuse from the law. It is the purpose of this chapter to investigate all those causes which excuse from the obligation of hearing Mass on Sundays and Feast-days. It will consider in order: ignorance, doubt, physical inability and moral inability. As a conclusion, the added but pertinent questions of the lawfulness of placing, and of the obligation of removing, causes which impede the fulfillment of the precept will be treated.

ARTICLE I. IGNORANCE AS AN EXCUSING CAUSE

Ignorance may be defined for our purposes as a lack of due knowledge, that is, a lack of knowledge of something which one could and should know. The conclusions and principles set down in this chapter as applicable to ignorance will be equally applicable to inadvertence and error, inasmuch as these are equivalent to ignorance when there is question of determining the obligation of a merely ecclesiastical law.

Ignorance may be either ignorance of law, or ignorance of fact. Ignorance of law exists when the existence, nature, comprehension or extension of a law is not known. Ignorance of fact exists when some fact or circumstance relative to the application or fulfillment of the law is not known. To illustrate: a person who does not know that a certain day is a day of precept is in ignorance of law; a person who knows that December 8th is a Feastday, but who does not know that the current day is December 8th is in ignorance of fact. The principles and conclusions which will be enunciated in this article apply to ignorance of fact as well as to ignorance of law.

Ignorance, whether it be of law or of fact, may be either invincible or vincible.

(a) Invincible Ignorance

A person is in invincible ignorance if he does not even suspect the existence of an obligation, or if, suspecting it, he is unaware that he must take means to find out the truth, or finally, if his use of such moral diligence as is proportionate to the gravity of the obligation concerned would not suffice to dispel his ignorance. Invincible ignorance is always inculpable and excuses from the law.[1] Therefore those would be excused from the precept of hearing Mass who do not know or advert to the fact that they must hear Mass on a certain prescribed day, or who, suspecting that they must hear Mass, are unaware of their obligation to investigate, or finally, those who, in order to ascertain the truth would have to resort to means which would entail notable inconvenience.

(b) Vincible Ignorance

In vincible ignorance there is always some measure of culpability. In order that a person be in vincible ignorance he must first suspect that an obligation exists and also realize that he has a duty to make further inquiry. If he refuses to make the inquiry, or uses less moral diligence to ascertain the truth than is demanded by the gravity of the obligation in question, then his ignorance is vincible. Such ignorance never excuses from the law, and hence it cannot be considered as an excusing cause. However it is of sufficient importance relative to the precept of hearing Mass to merit consideration here, for the culpable neglect which is always present in such ignorance is the basis for determining the gravity of the sin which is necessarily involved. It is very important to note that when there is question of vincible ignorance it makes no difference whether an obligation ac-

[1] Cf. Michiels, *Normae Generales*, I, 349.

tually exists or not. The sin consists not in the actual omission of the duty prescribed, but in the act of the will by which the person voluntarily exposes himself to the danger of sinning when he refuses to take the necessary means to ascertain his obligation.[2]

It has been stated that the degree of culpable neglect is the basis for determining the gravity of the sin committed by a person who is in vincible ignorance. Hence a person who voluntarily refuses to take the necessary means, lest by doing so he discover his obligation and be obliged to fulfill it, is in affected ignorance and commits a mortal sin. For example, a man suspects that a certain day is a Feastday and that he must consequently hear Mass. He is aware of his obligation to take measures to find out the truth, and knows that he can do so by consulting a Catholic paper which is at hand. He purposely neglects to consult the paper lest by doing so he be obliged to attend Mass. He commits a mortal sin whether or not the day in question is actually a Feastday for his sin consists in the malicious willingness to expose himself to mortal sin.

Similarly a person who, through sheer indifference, neglects to take any means whatsoever to ascertain the truth, or who makes only a slight effort which is notably improportionate to the gravity of the law in question, is in gravely culpable ignorance, and he also commits a mortal sin. To illustrate: a man suspects that he is bound to go to Mass on a certain day and is aware that he must take means to discover the truth. There are many means at his disposal by which he can find out whether or not the day is a Feastday, such as consulting the paper, calling his pastor on the telephone, etc. Through sheer indifference, however, he neglects to use any of these mans, or he contents himself with merely asking another member of his family who is equally uncertain. He commits a mortal sin because his neglect is gravely culpable.

Finally, a person who makes a genuine effort to ascertain the truth, but who neglects one or the other means which he could still use, with the result that his effort is not fully proportionate to the gravity of the obligation involved, is in lightly culpable ignorance and commits a venial sin proportionate to the degree of his neglect.

[2] Aertnys-Damen, *Theologia Moralis,* I, n. 51.

Thus a man who makes a sincere effort to find out whether or not a certain day is a Feastday, but who neglects one or the other means which he still could and should use, commits only a venial sin, because due to the sincere effort which he has already put forth his ignorance has become only lightly culpable.[3]

ARTICLE II. DOUBT AS AN EXCUSING CAUSE

(a) Positive and Objective Doubt of Law

Doubt may be defined as a state of mind withholding assent between two contradictory propositions. Doubt that is merely NEGATIVE, that is, doubt which exists when the mind has no reasons at all, or at least no reasons of any consequence, for adhering to either of the contradictory propositions may be dismissed as having no import with relation to the obligation of law. It is POSITIVE doubt, that is, doubt which exists in the mind because of reasons which are present in favor of each of the contradictory propositions, with which this article will be exclusively concerned.

Strict doubts exists when the reasons considered in support of each of the contradictory propositions so mutually balance each other that the mind must suspend judgment—it can assent to neither one nor the other. Moralists and canonists, however, extend the notion of positive doubt so as to include that state of mind which results when there is a compelling motive for assenting to one of the propositions but there is at the same time a prudent fear that the other proposition is true.[4]

Positive doubt may be either DOUBT of LAW or DOUBT of FACT. Doubt of law exists when there is a doubt concerning the existence, the force, the extent or the cessation of the law; doubt of fact, when the doubt concerns some fact or circumstance relative to the application or fulfillment of the law.

Furthermore, doubt, whether it be of law or of fact, can be SUBJECTIVE or OBJECTIVE. It is subjective when the doubt

[3] Cf. Michiels, *Normae Generales,* I, 348 ff.; Aertnys-Damen, *Theologia Moralis,* I, nn. 25-28; Cicognani, *Canon Law,* pp. 592-599; Maroto, *Institutiones Iuris Canonici,* I, n. 231. Cf. also canons 2199, 2202, 2203, 2229.

[4] Michiels, *Normae Generales,* I, 333; Cicognani, *Canon Law,* p. 587.

exists in the mind alone, having no basis in the nature of things. It is objective when there is something in the nature of things to correspond to the doubt that exists in the mind. Subjective doubt, since it does not exist outside the mind, is governed by the principles enunciated by moral theologians, as will be explained later in this article. It is of extreme importance to remember that the norm derived from canon 15 concerning a doubt of law, which will be immediately considered, is applicable to POSITIVE OBJECTIVE DOUBT ONLY! [5]

Canon 15: Leges, etiam irritantes et inhabilitantes, in dubio iuris non urgent; in dubio autem facti, potest Ordinarius in eis dispensare, dummodo agatur de legibus in quibus Romanus Pontifex dispensare solet.

By reason of the prescription of this canon it is now beyond dispute that when a positive and objective doubt exists concerning the existence, force, extent or cessation of a law, the law does not bind.[6] Canon 15 states simply "*Leges . . . in dubio iuris non urgent*"; and therefore it must be held that the law does not bind when there is a positive and objective doubt even as to its cessation. For this reason the principle as enunciated by St. Alphonsus,[7] which requires that in a positive doubt as to the cessation of the law the law must be observed, is not applicable when there is question of a positive OBJECTIVE doubt concerning the cessation of an ecclesiastical law.[8]

Applying this prescription of canon 15 to the specific subject of this study, it can be stated that whenever there is a positive and objective doubt concerning the existence, force, extent, or cessation of the precept of hearing Mass, there is no obligation to attend Mass. Hence, heretics and schismatics, whose obligation with regard to the precept is a matter of dispute among authors, can in practice be held as not bound by the law.

[5] Michiels, *Normae Generales,* I, 334; Cicognani, *Canon Law,* p. 587.

[6] Cf. Michiels, *loc. cit.*; Cicognani, *loc. cit.*

[7] *Theologia Moralis,* lib. I, n. 27.

[8] Cf. Wouters, *Manuale Theologia Moralis,* I, 178.

(b) Positive and Objective Doubt of Fact

Canon 15 further states that in a doubt of fact, that is, in a positive and objective doubt concerning some fact or circumstance relative to the application or fulfillment of the law, the ordinary can dispense, provided that the law is of a kind from which the Pope is accustomed to dispense. The restriction placed on the power of the ordinary by this canon is of no import here because by virtue of canon 1245 the ordinary, and even the pastor, can dispense from the observance of Feastdays. It is important to note that canon 15 states merely that the ordinary CAN dispense—it does not say that a dispensation is always necessary. It seems therefore that in the internal forum the probable opinions of moral theologians can safely be followed, unless the matter is one of great importance, in which case application should be made for a dispensation *ad cautelam.*[9]

Hence, with regard to the precept of hearing Mass, it seems safe, in a positive objective doubt of fact, to follow the norms laid down by moral theologians. It is evident, then, that the determination of the obligation in any given case will depend entirely upon what moral system is followed.

The present writer adheres to the moral system as proposed by St. Alphonsus. According to his system the following principles are applicable in a case which involves a positive objective doubt of fact.

(1) Non licet sequi opinionem minus probabilem pro libertate, relicta notabiliter seu certo probabiliori pro lege.

(2) Factum in dubio non praesumitur, sed probari debet:

(A) in dubio facti FUNDANTIS legem, possidet libertas;

(B) in dubio facti SUPPONENTIS legem, possidet lex;

(3) In dubio omne factum praesumitur recte factum.[10]

From the first principle, namely, that it is not permissible to follow a less probable opinion in favor of liberty, and to reject a notably more probable opinion in favor of the law, it is evident that a person who has some reasons to judge that he is free from the obliga-

[9] Maroto, *Institutiones Iuris Canonici,* I, n. 230; Cicognani, *Canon Law,* p. 590; Michiels, *Normae Generales,* I, 337.

[10] St. Alphonsus, *Theologia Moralis,* lib. I, nn. 54, 26, 27; Aertnys-Damen, *Theologia Moralis,* I, nn. 98, 71, 72.

tion of hearing Mass, but who has notably stronger reasons to judge that he is bound, is obliged to go to Mass.

According to the second principle, if a person doubts about a fact whose existence would induce an obligation in his regard, then he is not subject to the doubtfully binding law because liberty is in possession. In this case the doubt must be a strict doubt, that is, the reasons which favor liberty and those which favor the law must be equal or at least nearly equal, otherwise the first principle applies. To illustrate this principle, if a person doubts for good reasons as to the fact of his baptism, he is not bound by the precept of hearing Mass, because it is by the fact of baptism that the obligation of obeying ecclesiastical laws is induced. If, however, he doubts about some fact whose existence would cause the obligation of the law to cease in his regard, then the law is still in possession and he is bound to observe it. For example, a person doubts whether the distance which he must travel in order to go to Mass is sufficient to constitute an excusing cause. If *de facto* the distance were great enough, the obligation of the precept would cease. Therefore, his doubt concerns some fact which would cause the cessation of the obligation of the law in his regard. He is obliged to go to Mass. One exception in the application of this principle must be noted. If a person is sick, and doubts whether his sickness is sufficiently serious to excuse him from the obligation of going to Mass, but is unable to secure a dispensation, he should first consult his doctor, or some other prudent man. If the doubt remains even after such consultation, he may consider himself as free from the obligation, because in this particular case, since there is danger of grave physical harm, the natural law of preserving one's health supersedes the ecclesiastical law.[11] In practice, according to the implications of this principle, one who doubts concerning a fact which would cause the cessation of the obligation of the law in his regard, must either go to Mass or apply for a dispensation.

The third principle states that in a doubt everything that has been done is presumed to have been rightly done, that is, if a principle act has been performed, and a doubt arises as to some circum-

[11] St. Alphonsus, *Theologia Moralis,* lib. III, n. 325; Aertnys-Damen, *Theologia Moralis,* I, n. 71.

stance, or necessary condition, or the manner in which it was performed, then it may be presumed that the act has been performed correctly. There is no obligation to repeat the principal act when such a doubt is present. Hence, a person who has already assisted at Mass on a Feastday, but who doubts whether he did so with the proper intention, is not bound to go to another Mass because the presumption is that he performed the prescribed act in the proper manner.

Not all readers of this study will subscribe to the opinions given above, for not all follow the moral system supported by St. Alphonsus. It is perfectly within their right to apply the principles of that approved system to which they adhere. Hence, the probabilists may excuse a person from the obligation in all those cases in which a truly probable opinion is had in favor of liberty, even though the opinion in favor of the law is notably more probable.

(c) Positive and Subjective Doubt of Law

In the first part of this article it was stated that the norm of canon 15 relative to a doubt of law can be applied only when the doubt of law is positive and OBJECTIVE. When the doubt of law is positive but merely SUBJECTIVE, that is, when it has no basis in the nature of things but exists only in the mind, then recourse must be had to the principles laid down by moral theologians. Once again the present writer adheres to the principles enunciated by St. Alphonsus, namely,

(1) *Lex in dubio de eius existentia seu promulgatione non obligat;*
(2) *Lex in dubio de eius cessatione obligat.*

These principles are based on the fundamental principle that *in dubio melior est conditio possidentis.* When the existence or promulgation of a law is doubted, then liberty is in possession and the law does not bind. When the cessation of the law is doubted, then the law is in possession and continues to bind until its cessation is proved.[12]

[12] St. Alphonsus, *Theologia Moralis,* lib. I, nn. 26, 63; Aertnys-Damen, *Theologia Moralis,* I, n. 68.

According to the first principle, therefore, when a person has a positive but merely subjective doubt as to the existence of the precept of hearing Mass, then he is not bound to hear Mass. For example, a *peregrinus* doubts as to whether he is obliged to hear Mass on a Feastday which is prescribed for the territory in which he happens to be. There can be no objective doubt concerning this matter, for *peregrini* are *de facto* not bound by such a territorial law. Hence his doubt is purely subjective, and he is not bound to go to Mass. On the other hand, the second principle states that if the doubt concerns the cessation of the law, then the person is bound to observe it. It cannot be stressed too strongly that here only SUBJECTIVE doubts are being considered; the norm to be applied when objective doubts are involved has been given at the beginning of this article. Thus, if a person doubts for reasons which exist merely in his own mind whether a certain day has been abrogated as a Feastday, he is bound to go to Mass.

Article III. Physical Inability as an Excusing Cause

The following principle is unanimously accepted by theologians: Any moderately grave cause, that is, one which involves some notable inconvenience, or some notable harm or danger to one's own goods of body or soul, or to those of one's neighbor, suffices to excuse one from the precept of hearing Mass.[18]

This norm is too general and indeterminate for practical use. Therefore all authors apply it to specific cases. While they resort to various forms of subdivision in doing so, they arrive in general at the same conclusions. Some apply it under the headings of *"impotentia, charitas, officium et consuetudo"*; others under *"impotentia physica,*

[18] St. Alphonsus, *Theologia Moralis,* lib. III, n. 324; Lehmkuhl, *Theologia Moralis,* I, 339; Wouters, *Manuale Theologiae Moralis,* I, 482; Prümmer, *Manuale Theologiae Moralis,* II, n. 486; Aertnys-Damen, *Theologia Moralis,* I, n. 530; Noldin-Schmitt, *De Praeceptis,* n. 263; Davis, *Moral and Pastoral Theology,* II, 64; Vermeersch, *Theologia Moralis,* III, n. 861; Sabetti-Barrett, *Compendium Theologiae Moralis,* n. 249; Merkelbach, *Summa Theologiae Moralis,* II, n. 703; Iorio, *Theologia Moralis,* II, n. 138; Kenrick, F. P., *Theologia Moralis* (3 vols., Philadelphiae, 1841-1843), I, 197; Coronata, *De Locis et Temporibus Sacris,* n. 292.

impotentia spiritualis, impotentia moralis." In this study, however, the more specific application of the general norm will be made under two headings, namely, under "*impotentia physica*" and "*impotentia moralis,*" because all the excusing causes admitted by authors can be classified under one of these titles.

Since practically all authors agree on the excusing causes which will be enumerated under each of the headings chosen, there will be no need of citing authors for each one. If any real dispute exists as to any one cause listed below, note will be made of it.

(a) *Kinds of Physical Inability*

Under this heading will be grouped all those excusing causes which directly affect the body of the subject himself, and thus render it impossible for him to go to Mass, or which involve some notable physical inconvenience or harm sufficient to release him from the obligation of attending Mass.

(1) Sickness or infirmity. This may be of such a nature as to render the going to Mass either an impossibility, or a source of notable inconvenience or of notable physical harm. Therefore, the following are excused:

Those who are bed-ridden or who are unable to walk; convalescents who prudently fear notable harm to their health, or even notable delay in their complete recovery; those who are advanced in years for whom the going to Mass would involve notable inconvenience or loss of strength; those who prudently fear that the going to Mass would cause severe headache or notable weakness. It is morally impossible to include here all the causes which would excuse one from the obligation. The ones just listed, however, may serve as a norm for judging other unlisted cases which may arise. With regard to convalescents a safe rule to follow is this: If they are not accustomed to leave the house for other reasons, they are not obliged to leave it in order to go to Mass.

(2) Physical impossibility of leaving the place in which one is. This would include those who are in prison, provided that no facilities for hearing Mass are available; those who are on a ship at sea; those who are on a train or on other vehicle which they cannot leave; and those who are in other similar circumstances. All these

causes excuse, provided that they were placed licitly according to the norms which will be given later in this study[14]

(3) Notable inconvenience which the going to Mass would involve. Under this type of excusing cause would be included:

Those who live at a great distance from the place where they could hear Mass. It is difficult to state absolutely just what distance would be sufficient to constitute an excusing cause, since the circumstances of time, place, person, weather, etc., must all be taken into consideration. Thus, for the young and strong a longer distance would be required than would suffice for the old or feeble. Similarly, for a person making the journey to Mass over smooth roads in mild and pleasant weather, a longer distance would be required than would suffice for one making it over difficult roads in rain or snow or cold weather. Some authors estimate that a distance of about three miles, or one which would require a good hour's walk (*i. e.*, a walk of about an hour and a quarter) would suffice if the journey has to be made on foot.[15]

Presumably the authors cited above propose their norm as one which is to be applied for normal persons under normal circumstances. Therefore due allowance should be made for extraordinary circumstances of person, place, etc., in applying it.

To the mind of the present writer the norm requiring 1¼ hours' walk seems a bit too strict in view of modern circumstances. The present generation is unaccustomed to walking and, due to that fact, a walk of more than one hour probably constitutes a notable inconvenience for most persons today. Therefore the present writer is inclined to think that a distance which requires more than an hour's walk suffices as an excusing cause. This opinion is not authoritative, but merely a venture on the part of the present writer, and should be weighed as such.

(b) Use of the Automobile

Those who have automobiles or other means of conveyance are, of course, bound to use them in order to fulfill the precept, and when

[14] Cf. Art. V of this chapter.

[15] Marc-Gestermann, *Institutiones*, I, n. 681; Aertnys-Damen, *Theologia Moralis*, I, n. 530; Davis, *Moral and Pastoral Theology*, II, 65.

they are used the distance required to constitute an excusing cause becomes proportionately greater. Kenrick states that those who travel by horse or carriage are not always excused even when they have to travel ten miles in this manner. No standard authors take travel by automobile into consideration. J. Nevins, however, in an article in the *Ecclesiastical Review,* estimates that a distance of fifteen miles would be the maximum requirement by this mode of travel, saying that that distance would be the equivalent of an hour and a quarter's ride.[16]

If Nevins' estimate is accepted as a reasonable norm, which it probably was at the time he wrote his article, then, in view of the notable improvements made in automobiles as well as in roads since 1928, it seems that the distance today required would be at least twenty miles. However, it is the opinion of this writer that the better norm to follow, and one which would be applicable in all localities, is simply that a ride of one and a quarter hours would suffice to constitute an excusing cause. Certainly this cannot be said to be too strict, since moral theologians require a walk of one and a quarter hours, and travel by automobile certainly entails less inconvenience than travel on foot. Even in applying this norm, however, consideration must be taken of other items which might be involved, such as the items of expense, driving on icy roads, etc. Ultimately, whether or not an excusing cause exists will depend upon a prudent judgment formed after due consideration of all the circumstances.

Article IV. Moral Inability as an Excusing Cause

(a) Kinds of Moral Inability

In this article will be considered all those causes which are sufficient to excuse one from the precept of hearing Mass, but which do not entail physical impossibility or involve physical harm or inconvenience to the person himself. The following causes will excuse:

(1) Duty. This includes soldiers, policemen, detectives, watch-

[16] Nevins, "Mass-going and the Automobile," *Ecclesiastical Review* (formerly *The American Ecclesiastical Review,* Philadelphia, 1889—), LXXVIII (1928), 129.

men and others who cannot leave their post, and who cannot conveniently secure permission to leave in order to hear Mass. It includes also parents with small children, whom they cannot conveniently leave in the charge of others. If they can take the children to Mass with them, they are obliged to do so, unless they prudently fear the undue disturbance of others in church. If husband and wife are both at home, they should make some arrangement by which both would be enabled to go to Mass—one going to one Mass, the other to another.

Under the cause of duty can also be included those who are obliged to work on days when Mass is prescribed, if they cannot attend Mass without arousing grave indignation on the part of their employer, or risking the loss of their position, or suffering other notable harm or inconvenience. If such workers, because of their work, are obliged to miss Mass on every Sunday and Feastday they should seek other employment if they can obtain such readily and without notable diminution of pay. Finally, if those who have to work on a day when Mass is prescribed can attend Mass at an early hour without suffering notable inconvenience due to loss of sleep, they are obliged to do so.

(2) Charity. This cause includes those who are taking care of the sick, and who cannot conveniently secure in their place the services of another. Even if the services of another could be secured, the person in charge would not be obliged to go to Mass if his absence would cause undue sadness or anxiety on the part of the sick person.

The cause of charity also includes those whose presence is necessary to avert grave loss or damage to the property of others, as in time of fire, or flood, violent storms, etc.

(3) Probable occasion of sin to others. Therefore, they are excused who prudently fear that their going to Mass will be the occasion of another's blaspheming, or indulging in excessive drink, or committing serious theft, etc. Similarly, a girl who knows that her appearance at church will occasion illicit desires on the part of a young man whom she knows to be sinfully attracted to her. Finally, under this cause may be included wives and children who know that their going to Mass will occasion violent quarrels and discord in the family.

(4) Notable inconvenience or damage or notable financial loss, either to oneself or to others. Under this head are excused those who, by going to Mass, would have to postpone a journey and thereby lose the helpful companionship which they could have if they neglected Mass. This would hold only if the journey were long and tedious.

Excused also are those whose attendance at Mass would involve notable financial loss. Authors insist that only the loss of some extraordinary and transitory gain would suffice to constitute an excusing cause. However, it seems that also the financial condition of the person concerned must be taken into consideration. Hence for the poor the loss of a small sum might easily cause notable inconvenience and so might reasonably be considered as an excusing cause.

(5) Notable embarrassment or injury to one's good name. Thus, under this cause may be included women who lack decent clothes suitable to their state of life, or girls who have become noticeably pregnant through illicit intercourse. If such can go to Mass at another church where they are not known, and can do so without notable inconvenience or danger to their good name, they must do so. The noticeable pregnancy of married women is not usually sufficient to warrant their staying away from Mass. In some individual cases, where due to abnormal sensibility, a wife would suffer notable embarrassment because of her manifest state of pregnancy, she could be considered as having an excusing cause.

(6) Custom. Sometimes, by reason of custom in particular localities, a person may be excused from attending Mass for reasons which in themselves would not constitute an excusing cause. For example, in some localities it is the custom for a girl to remain away from Mass when the banns of her marriage are being announced. It need hardly be stated that such a girl is excused from attending only the Mass at which the banns are actually announced. If she can attend another Mass without notable inconvenience, she is bound to do so. In exceptional cases, girls may be excused on this score even in localities where such a custom does not exist, provided that their presence would cause them notable embarrassment.

In other places it is the custom for the immediate family of a deceased to remain away from Mass because of grief, or for mothers to remain away for a few weeks after childbirth. In all such cases, the respective persons would be excused from the precept, provided that they do not leave the house for other reasons, for example, to visit friends.

(7) Excommunication and interdict. *Vitandi* and those who are under personal interdict are forbidden to attend Mass; therefore, if they are actually under the censure and cannot obtain absolution they are excused from the obligation of attending Mass. However, as has been pointed out earlier in this study, if they can without grave inconvenience secure absolution but neglect to do so, they would not be excused from mortal sin. That is the opinion of the present writer. In view however of the probable doubt of law which exists, all excommunicates may probably be considered as excused from the precept.

(b) Use of Privilege to Fulfill Precept

A controverted question which arises in connection with excusing causes is this: Can those persons be considered excused from the obligation who on a Sunday or Feastday, can hear Mass only by availing themselves of some privilege which they enjoy? In other words, is a person obliged to use a privilege, such as that of a private oratory, or that of the portable altar, in order to fulfill the precept of hearing Mass?

Some authors excuse such persons on the plea that no one is bound to use a privilege in order to fulfill the precept, lest the privilege become a burden rather than a favor. They maintain that a person who can hear Mass on a Sunday or Feastday only by using his privilege of a private oratory or the portable altar, is excused from the precept.[17]

The better and more common opinion, however, seems to be that such persons are obliged to make use of their privilege in order to fulfill the precept of hearing Mass. Canon 69 states that no one is obliged to use a privilege which has been granted solely in his own favor, unless an obligation arises from some other source. Woywod

[17] Coronata, *De Locis et Temporibus Sacris*, n. 292; Woywod, *Commentary*, I, n. 51; Noldin-Schmitt, *De Principiis*, n. 195.

claims that the canon does not intend to include other laws of the Code among the "other sources of obligation." However, there seems to be no good reason for holding this opinion. This study adopts the opinion of those authors who hold that, if a person who enjoys a privilege cannot fulfill the precept of hearing Mass in any other way, he must make use of the privilege in order to fulfill his obligation, as long as he can do so without moderately grave inconvenience. Hence, a person who has the privilege of a private oratory must attend Mass there, if Mass is said, and must even arrange for Mass to be said, if he can do so without notable inconvenience or expense, because one who is bound by an obligation must take the means at his disposel to fulfill it.[18]

Article V. The Placing and Removal of Causes Impeding the Fulfillment of the Precept

It will be appropriate to consider in this chapter the question of when it is lawful to place, and obligatory to remove, causes which interfere with or impede the fulfillment of the precept of hearing Mass. Before this question can be answered, however, certain fundamental concepts must be clarified.

A cause may be either an exempting cause, or merely an impeding or excusing cause. An exempting cause is one which removes a person from the jurisdiction of the law, and renders him no longer subject to it. An excusing cause is one which prevents a person from fulfilling a law to which he is actually and truly subject. Each of these causes may be present, proximate or remote, depending upon whether it is placed at a time when the law has actually begun to bind, or at a time shortly before the law begins to bind, or at a time considerably before the law begins to bind. Again, each of these

[18] St. Alphonsus, *Theologia Moralis,* lib. III, n. 324; Cicognani, *Canon Law,* p. 807; Aertnys-Damen, *Theologia Moralis,* I, n. 215; Marc-Gestermann, *Institutiones,* I, n. 251; Maroto, *Institutiones Iuris Canonici,* I, n. 300, A, b; Roelker, *Principles of Privilege According to the Code of Canon Law,* The Catholic University of American Canon Law Studies, n. 35 (Washington, D. C., The Catholic University of America, 1926), p. 95, footnote n. 28.

causes can be placed directly, that is, for the precise purpose of evading the law, or indirectly, that is, for some other motive, although the evasion of the law is foreseen.

(a) Lawfulness of Placing Such Causes

With these concepts clarified, certain general principles may now be enunciated:

(1) It is lawful to directly place an exempting cause, even after the law has actually begun to bind. This follows from the fact that, while a person has an obligation to fulfill a law to which he is subject, he has no obligation to remain subject to a law if he can withdraw himself from its jurisdiction. If the law has already begun to bind, however, then the exempting cause must be placed before the last opportunity of fulfilling the precept presents itself.

Thus a person can lawfully place a remote, proximate or present cause which exempts him from the precept of hearing Mass, even with the precise intention of evading the law. For example, a person can lawfully leave a territory where the hearing of Mass is prescribed and go into another territory where it is not prescribed even if he does so in order not to be obliged to go to Mass. He may leave a week before the day on which the obligation binds, or a day before, or even on the morning of the day itself, but in the latter case, he must be out of the territory before the time of the last Mass which he could hear has arrived.[19]

(2) It is never lawful to place an excusing cause directly, that is, for the precise purpose of evading the obligation. The reason is that, so long as a person is subject to a law, he cannot directly will to violate it.

Thus a person can never lawfully place a cause which will excuse him from hearing Mass, precisely in order that he may evade the law, even if the cause is remote. To illustrate: A person cannot law-

[19] Marc-Gestermann, *Institutiones,* I, n. 225; Tanquerey, *Synopsis Theologiae Moralis,* II, n. 305; Konings, *Theologia Moralis,* n. 110; Maroto, *Institutiones Iuris Canonici,* I, nn. 202, 228, 233; Aertnys-Damen, *Theologia Moralis,* I, n. 151; Noldin-Schmitt, *De Principiis,* n. 152.

fully, even on the preceding Monday, go to a place which is far removed from a church, solely for the purpose of being excused from hearing Mass on the following Sunday.[20]

(3) It is not lawful even indirectly to place an excusing cause which is present or proximate, unless there is a proportionate reason for doing so.

Thus, if the precept of hearing Mass has already begun to bind, or will begin to bind shortly, a person may not lawfully place an excusing cause even for a purpose other than the evasion of the law, unless he has a proportionate reason for doing so. For example, a person cannot lawfully start out on a journey on Sunday morning without first hearing Mass, nor can he lawfully start out on a journey on Saturday, if he foresees that he will miss Mass the following day because of it, unless he has a reason proportionate to the gravity of the precept for making such a journey, *e. g.*, to go to the bedside of a dying relative.

The basis of this principle, no doubt, is that usually the postponement, for a few hours or for a day, of the placing of a cause which would excuse from the precept does not involve moderately grave inconvenience. If the postponement of placing the cause would *de facto* entail moderately grave inconvenience, then this in itself would constitute an excusing cause, and would therefore certainly supply the proportionate reason as demanded by the principle.[21]

(4) It is lawful to place a remote excusing cause indirectly, even without a special reason.

Thus, a person can lawfully place an excusing cause for some reason other than the evasion of the precept of hearing Mass, as long as he does so a few days before the precept begins to bind. For example, he can start out on a journey certainly on Thursday, and probably even on Friday, as long as his motive in doing so is not precisely that of being excused from Mass on the following Sunday.[22]

[20] Marc-Gestermann, *Institutiones,* I, n. 225; Merkelbach, *Summa Theologiae Moralis,* I, n. 379.

[21] Marc-Gestermann, *loc. cit.*; Merkelbach, *loc. cit.*

[22] Aertnys-Damen, *Theologia Moralis,* I, n. 184; Marc-Gestermann, *Institutiones,* I, n. 225; Merkelbach, *Summa Theologiae Moralis,* I, n. 379.

Authors, in stating this principle, give as the reason behind it the fact that it would be gravely burdensome to abstain from placing causes which would impede a law, when the law will not begin to bind for a considerable time. It is no doubt true that usually such abstention from placing remote causes would entail moderately grave inconvenience.

However, it is possible that in particular instances the placing of an excusing cause, however remote, can be postponed without any inconvenience whatsoever. It is the opinion of the writer that, when this can be done, then the principle as here stated under n. 4 cannot lawfully be invoked, because the basis underlying it is no longer verified. For example, a man wishes to take a pleasure trip. He can start either on Thursday and thereby be compelled to miss Mass on the following Sunday, or he can start the following Monday and thereby be able to attend Sunday Mass before he goes. He is absolutely indifferent as to when he starts, for he is equally satisfied with starting on either day. It seems to the writer that in such circumstances the man is obliged to postpone the start of his trip till Monday, in order that he may be able to fulfill his Sunday Mass obligation, even though the placing of the excusing cause on Thursday would constitute only a remote impediment to the fulfillment of the precept.

(b) Obligation of Removing Such Causes

The next question to be considered is: When is it obligatory to remove causes which already exist? In general the principles regulating the lawfulness of placing causes may also be applied to determine the obligation of removing such as already exist. Thus

(1) There is never an obligation to remove a cause which exempts one from the precept, even if one's sole purpose in neglecting to remove it is to evade the law. Hence, a *peregrinus* is not obliged to return to his own territory in order to fulfill the precept of hearing Mass which is in force there, even if he wishes to remain away precisely in order not to have to attend Mass.

(2) It is never lawful to neglect the removal of an excusing cause for the precise motive of evading the law. For example, a

person cannot remain in a place which is far removed from a church, if his sole motive in doing so is precisely to be excused from the precept.

(3) It is not lawful to neglect removing the cause if the law has already begun to bind, or will begin to bind shortly, unless a proportionate reason is had to warrant the neglect. For example, if a person who lives more than three miles from a church can borrow a neighbor's car and thus remove the excusing cause which is realized in his regard, he is obliged to do so. If, however, for not doing so he has reasons which are proportionate to the gravity of the precept of hearing Mass, he is excused from removing the cause. Such reasons are present, for example, when the borrowing of the car would put the owner to a great deal of trouble, or would cause great displeasure or resentment on his part.

(4) It is difficult to enunciate any definite principle which would serve as a practical norm by which to determine the obligation of removing impeding causes which are remote. Most remote causes eventually become proximate and present. It seems that the obligation of removing remote causes can best be determined on the basis of the inconvenience involved in their removal. If the removal involves notable inconvenience, then the person may be considered as excused, but if the removal occasions little or no inconvenience then the person must remove even a remote cause. For example, suppose a person can remove an impeding cause four or five days before the precept of hearing Mass will begin to bind, but will be unable to do so at a more proximate time. Usually the removal of such a cause so far in advance entails notable inconvenience, and the person, as a rule, has no obligation to do so. However, if in some particular instance a person can remove such a cause that far in advance with little or no inconvenience, it is the opinion of the writer that he has an obligation to do so. Thus, a person who is in a place which is far distant from a church is not usually bound to depart from that place four or five days in advance in order to be able to attend Mass the following Sunday. But if such a person, who will be unable to leave later on in the week, can leave on Tuesday or Wednesday with little or no inconvenience, he is obliged to do so in order that he may attend Mass on the following Sunday.

(c) Obligation When a Later Impeding Cause Is Foreseen

A final question remains to be considered. If a person foresees that he will later be impeded from fulfilling the precept of hearing Mass, is he bound to fulfill it at a time when he is able to do so?

Once again the distinction between exempting causes and excusing causes must be made. If a person foresees that he will later be exempted from the precept, he is under no obligation to fulfill it before he becomes exempt. For example, if a person foresees that he will have left the territory where Mass is prescribed before the time of the last Mass arrives, he is not obliged to go to Mass before he departs. If, however, a person foresees that later a cause will arise which will merely excuse him from the precept, then he is obliged to fulfill it before the excusing cause is realized. Hence, a mother who foresees that she will be unable to attend the 11 o'clock Mass because of the children, is obliged to go to an earlier Mass if she can leave the children to the father's care during that time.[23]

It is to be understood in these cases, of course, that the precept has already begun to bind. There is no obligation whatsoever of anticipating a law which has not as yet begun to bind. Therefore, no one is obliged to go to Mass on Saturday morning simply because he foresees that he will be unable to go on Sunday.

[23] Aertnys-Damen, *Theologia Moralis,* I, n. 185; Maroto, *Institutiones Iuris Canonici,* I, n. 208; Marc-Gestermann, *Institutiones,* I, n. 226.

CHAPTER XIII

DISPENSATION FROM THE PRECEPT OF HEARING MASS

Canon 1245, § 1: Non solum Ordinarii locorum, sed etiam parochi, in casibus singularibus iustaque de causa, possunt subiectos sibi singulos fideles singulasve familias, etiam extra territorium, atque in suo territorio etiam peregrinos, a lege communi de observantia festorum . . . dispensare.

§ 3: In religione clericali exempta eandem dispensandi potestatem habent Superiores ad modum parochi, quod attinet ad personas, de quibus in can. 514, § 1.

CANON 1245, in paragraphs one and three, grants to local ordinaries, pastors and superiors of clerical exempt religious institutes a certain restricted power of dispensing from the precept of hearing Mass. It is the purpose of this chapter to investigate this power in order to determine those who may exercise it, those in whose favor it may be used, and the conditions necessary for its legitimate exercise.

ARTICLE I. ACTIVE SUBJECT OF THE POWER OF DISPENSING

Canon 1245, in paragraph 1, states that not only local ordinaries but also pastors can dispense from the common law which prescribes the observance of Feastdays; the same canon, in paragraph 3, extends to superiors of clerical exempt religious institutes a like power, to be used by them after the manner of in which pastors can exercise it. Therefore the following enjoy the power to dispense from the precept of hearing Mass as enjoined by common law: all local ordinaries as enumerated in canon 198, including their vicars-general; all pastors, together with those who are equivalent to pastors according to canon 451, § 2; and all superiors of clerical exempt religious institutes, including local superiors.

This power, since it is attached to the respective office by the law itself, is to be considered as ordinary power.[1] Accordingly it may be delegated to another either totally or in part, since the law makes no special provision to the contrary.[2] Furthermore, because it is a non-judicial power of jurisdiction, those who possess it may exercise it in their own favor, they may exercise it when they themselves are outside their own proper territory, and they may exercise it in favor of their own subjects who are absent from their proper territory.[3]

Confessors, as such, have no power to dispense from the precept of hearing Mass, unless it has been delegated to them. In the absence of such a delegation, they may at most declare an excusing cause to be present in a given case. Similarly, superiors of religious institutes which are not clerical exempt may not dispense their subjects from the precept unless they have received this power through delegation. Hence they must apply for such a dispensation either to the ordinary or to the pastor.

It is important to note that the power granted by canon 1245 is a power merely of dispensing. Those who enjoy it, therefore, may not commute the obligation of hearing Mass into some other obligation. The reason why they cannot do so is this: The commutation of an obligation which arises from common law is equivalent to the enactment of a new law, and the Code cannot be considered as conceding legislative power to him to whom it grants the power of merely relaxing the obligation.[4] Consequently those who dispense from the precept of bearing Mass may urge the substitution of some other pious work, but may not prescribe it as a substitute duty.

Finally, since the obligation of hearing Mass is indivisible, those who dispense must dispense from the entire obligation of hearing Mass and not just from a portion of it.[5]

[1] Canon 197, § 1.

[2] Canon 199, § 1.

[3] Canon 201, § 3.

[4] Vermeersch-Creusen, *Epitome*, II, n. 553.

[5] Coronata, *De Locis et Temporibus Sacris*, n. 278.

Article II. Passive Subject of the Power of Dispensing

According to canon 1245, § 1, local ordinaries and pastors can dispense individuals and single families who are subject to them, even when these are outside their proper territory, and also *peregrini* who are within the territory of the local ordinaries and pastors. It is important to note that the canon gives to pastors the identical power which it gives to local ordinaries. The local ordinary's power is greater only in so far as he can exercise it over a greater number of subjects and throughout a greater extent of territory. However, in its actual exercise he is restricted by the very same limitations as is the pastor, namely, he can use it in favor only of individuals and of single families subject to him.

Some authors propose that since the parish is to a local ordinary what the family is to a pastor, the local ordinary may use this faculty to dispense whole parishes.[6] This conclusion seems hardly justifiable in the light of canon 18, which states that ecclesiastical laws are to be understood according to the proper meaning of the words considered in their text and context. To say the least, the interpretation of the word *familia* to signify "parish" when it clearly signifies "family" and nothing more, is an undue distortion of its meaning. Coronata justifies his interpretation by arguing: In consideration of the proportion existing between the local ordinary and the pastor, one must conclude that the former can dispense whole portions of his territory, or else be forced to say that the pastor has greater power than he. Apparently Coronata means greater power, relatively considered, because *de facto* the pastor has only the same power, namely, to dispense individuals and single families. If, as Coronata seems to claim, it is necessary, or even only fitting, that the ordinary possess more power than the pastor in consideration of the proportion existing between them, it may be suggested that he actually has, in so far as he can exercise it over a greater number of individuals and a greater number of single families. For want of better reasons to support it, the opinion that ordinaries can dispense whole parishes by virtue of canon 1245, § 1, may be rejected as improbable.[7]

[6] *E.g.*, Coronata, *De Locis et Temporibus Sacris*, n. 276.

[7] Vermeersch-Creusen, *Epitome*, II, n. 554.

If some just cause should arise which would demand the dispensation of the entire diocese from the precept of hearing Mass, then the local ordinary could concede such a dispensation, provided that recourse to the Holy See would be difficult and that there would be present at the same time danger of grave harm if the grant of the dispensation were delayed. He could do this, not indeed by virtue of canon 1245, § 1, but by virtue of canon 81.[8]

Both the local ordinary and the pastor can dispense individuals and single families subject to them. They cannot dispense a group of individuals or a number of families as such. However, if the one empowered to dispense knows that a cause sufficient for dispensation is truly had by all the individuals in a group, it is probable that by one act he could give a dispensation which would virtually touch each individual, just as if he had granted it by separate successive acts.[9]

Vermeersch-Creusen maintain that a local ordinary could also dispense a single family for a cause common to it, even though the cause did not affect each individual member.[10] It is difficult to understand precisely what Vermeersch-Creusen mean by this observation, and why they specify the local ordinary as if to exclude the pastor. The precept of hearing Mass binds not the family as a family, but each individual as an individual, and for this reason it seems only logical to conclude that each individual member must be affected by the warranting cause before the ordinary or pastor can grant a family dispensation. With regard to other laws of the Church it is possible to envision a cause which is common to a family and justifies the grant of a common dispensation, even though each individual of the family is not directly affected by the cause in question. Thus, if two members of a family, for example, have a sufficient cause to be dispensed from the law of abstinence, the ordinary or pastor could at times, no doubt, dispense the entire family in view of the difficulty of preparing distinct meals. It is difficult, however, to imagine a cause which would warrant a dispensation

[8] Coronata, *op. cit.,* n. 276.

[9] Vermeersch-Creusen, *loc. cit.*

[10] Vermeersch-Creusen, *loc. cit.*

from the precept of hearing Mass for an entire family, but which does not directly affect each member thereof.

Canon 1245, § 1, states that the local ordinary or pastor can dispense his subjects *"etiam extra territorium."* These words refer both to the one dispensing, who may wish, while absent from his proper territory, to dispense his subjects, and also to the subjects themselves who are outside their own territory and who may wish to secure a dispensation from their proper local ordinary or pastor. Furthermore, there is no good reason why a local ordinary or pastor may not send, from a place other than his own territory, a dispensation to a *peregrinus* or a *vagus* who is at the time residing in the territory of the grantor.[11]

Canon 1245, § 1, continues by stating that the local ordinary or pastor can dispense *"in suo territorio etiam peregrinos."* The words *"in suo territorio"* can be referred only to the one granting the dispensation, since in order to be a peregrinus one must be outside one's own proper territory. These words, therefore, signify that the local ordinary or pastor can exercise his power on only those *peregrini* who are within his diocese or parish. A dispensation given to a *peregrinus* by a local ordinary or pastor is a personal grant, since it is given to an individual in view of a special cause peculiar to that individual.[12] Therefore the phrase *"in suo territorio"* restricts only the use of jurisdiction, and not the use of the dispensation. The *peregrinus* may use the dispensation even outside the territory of the local ordinary or pastor from whom he obtained it.[13]

Canon 1245, § 3, grants to superiors of exempt clerical religious institutes the same power to dispense from the precept of hearing Mass as it grants to pastors, to be exercised in favor of all those persons who are enumerated in canon 514, § 1. Hence they may dispense not only the professed and the novices, but also other persons who dwell day and night in the religious house, whether as servants,

[11] Vermeersch-Creusen, *Epitome,* II, n. 554; canon 201, § 3.

[12] Reilly, Edward M., *The General Norms of Dispensation,* The Catholic University of America Canon Law Studies, n. 119 (Washington, D. C.: The Catholic University of America Press, 1939), p. 105.

[13] Vermeersch-Creusen, *Epitome,* II, n. 554; Michiels, *Normae Generales,* II, 462.

as guests, as convalescents, or for the purpose of education. They may also dispense visiting religious who are staying in the house, for these may be considered a *peregrini.*

The rector of a seminary, or his delegate, has the same power of dispensing as has a pastor, and he can use it with regard to all those who are in the seminary. This appears evident from canon 1368, which states that the seminary is exempt from parochial jurisdiction, and that the rector or his delegate exercises the office of pastor toward all those who are in the seminary. If the Holy See has determined otherwise with regard to a particular seminary, then of course, the rector does not enjoy such power.

Canon 1245, § 3, states that the superiors of clerical exempt religious institutes can exercise their power to dispense *"ad modum parochi."* The pastor may exercise it in favor of individuals and single families. The question arises, then, as to whether the religious superior's power is restricted solely to individuals, since families, as a rule, are not to be found in religious houses. The proper meaning of the word *"familia"* is "family" and hence it appears that the religious superior's power is so restricted. However, it seems probable that the superiors in question can exercise their power in favor of the entire community, if the community is small, or in favor of distinct minor units of the community, if it is large. The reason is this: the superior's power can be exercised *"ad modum parochi"* and if it were restricted to individuals, then it would not correspond to the power as exercised by pastors. Furthermore, small communities, at least, and minor units of communities can be considered as the equivalent of families since they live under a common roof, partake of the same meals, receive common support and depend upon the same superiors. Thus, the analogy between a family and a religious community is much closer than the analogy between a family and an entire diocese or parish, and this explains why the present writer inclines to the opinion that superiors can dispense the groups in question, while he denies that bishops or pastors can dispense entire dioceses or parishes. Another reason for admitting this power on the part of the religious superiors is that a common cause which affects each member of the community or unit can arise and be easily recognized. Such a cause could not so easily arise or be recognized in regard to an entire diocese or parish. Therefore, it may be asserted as at least probable, that religious superiors of exempt clerical institutes can dispense the entire community, if it is small, and the minor units of large communities when a cause warranting such a dispensation is present.[14]

Article III. Conditions Required for the Granting of a Dispensation

(a) "In Casibus Singularibus"

Canon 1245, § 1, states that the local ordinary or pastor can dispense *"in casibus singularibus iustaque de causa."* The power therefore is restricted to individual cases and may be exercised only when a just cause is present.

Some authors interpret the phrase *"in casibus singularibus"* as referring to the individual subjects of the grantor of the dispensation.[15] This can hardly be its meaning, however, since the canon itself, immediately after the phrase in question, uses the words *"subiectos sibi singulos fideles."* It is hardly possible that the Code would use two different phrases to convey the very same idea.

The better opinion is that it signifies an individual case as opposed to a plurality of cases. An individual case is determined as such by the cause which is present with regard to the subject, and which warrants the grant of the dispensation. If the cause is of such a nature that it endures for only one Sunday or Feastday, then the dispensation, which is given in the "individual case" as determined by that cause, may be granted for only the one Sunday or Feastday concerned. If, however, the cause is of such a nature that it will endure for an extended period of time, then the "individual case" will include the same period, and a dispensation can be granted which will cover all Sundays and Feastdays occurring within that period of time. For example, a person wishes to make an exploration trip which will cover the period of a month. The

[14] Cf. Vermeersch-Creusen, *Epitome*, II, n. 556; Coronata, *De Locis et Temporibus Sacris*, n. 280.

[15] Coronata, *De Locis et Temporibus Sacris*, n. 276.

cause is the trip, and since the cause endures for a month, the "individual case" which it determines endures for a month together with it. The ordinary may dispense, therefore, in the "individual case" in question, and his dispensation will be valid for all the Sundays and Feastdays occurring within that period.[16]

As has been stated, an "individual case" is opposed to a plurality of cases, which is also determined by the cause, or rather, causes. A plurality of cases exists when an individual is affected by two or more distinct causes in view of which he wishes to obtain a dispensation from correspondingly distinct obligations. The local ordinary or pastor cannot with a single dispensation relax all the existing obligations. For example, a person wishes to make three trips on successive week-ends, each for a different reason. The ordinary or pastor could not grant one dispensation to cover all three Sundays.

(b) "Iusta de Causa"

Canon 1245, § 1, states that the ordinary or pastor must have a just cause in order to dispense from the precept of hearing Mass. It is impossible to determine exactly how grave a cause must be in order to constitute a just cause for a dispensation relative to the precept of hearing Mass. This much is certain: A less grave cause suffices for a dispensation than is required for excusing one from the precept. Since any moderately grave cause excuses from the precept of hearing Mass provided that it involves notable inconvenience or considerable harm, a just cause for dispensation can be one which is less than moderately grave. On the other hand, however, it must not be so light as to be entirely out of proportion to the gravity of the precept of hearing Mass. In any given case, it is left to the prudent judgment of the grantor of the dispensation to decide whether a just cause is present in relation to the gravity of the precept.[17]

Local ordinaries and pastors, then, must prudently judge that a just cause exists before they can grant a dispensation. If they grant a dispensation for a cause which certainly is not just and reasonable,

[16] Michiels, *Normae Generales*, II, 515; Vermeersch-Creusen, *Epitome*, II, n. 554.

[17] Vermeersch-Creusen, *Epitome*, I, n. 196.

then the dispensation is illicit and invalid. If they dispense in a doubt as to whether the cause is sufficient, the dispensation is licit and valid.[18]

Before the Code pastors could dispense from the precept of hearing Mass only for an urgent cause. Under the present law the cause required for pastors is the same as that which is required for local ordinaries, as is evident from canon 1245, § 1, which makes no distinction between them. The cause for pastors, therefore, need no longer be urgent; it need only be just.[19]

The same limitations which have here been considered apply to the power of dispensing as enjoyed by superiors of exempt clerical institutes by reason of canon 1245, § 3, for they may exercise their power only *"ad modum parochi."* Rectors of seminaries, since they exercise the office of pastor with regard to those living in the seminary, are likewise held to the same restrictions.

[18] Canon 84.

[19] St. Alphonsus, *Theologia Moralis,* lib. III, n. 388.

CONCLUSIONS

THE following opinions are offered as conclusions resulting from the present study. If the conclusions are not entirely new, they have become perhaps better established as the result of new arguments adduced in their support.

(1) The Sunday was adopted by the early Christians in substitution for the Sabbath, not by reason of divine positive law, but by reason of custom which grew out of the circumstances of the times.

(2) The first written law which prescribed attendance at Sunday Mass was not canon 21 of the Council of Elvira (306), as many authors suppose, but more probably canon 47 of the Council of Agde (506).

(3) Before the middle of the thirteenth century the obligation of attending Sunday Mass in the parish church existed, but was not insisted upon by the Councils because it was conscientiously observed.

(4) The precept of hearing Mass on Sundays and Feastdays arises solely from merely ecclesiastical law (pp. 67-68).

(5) The prescription of canon 1247, § 3, does not apply to previous abrogations made by universal law, but only to previous abrogations made by particular law (pp. 77-79).

(6) Subjects of the obligation arising from a territorial Feastday may leave the territory in order to evade the local obligation provided that they will be outside the territory before the time of the last Mass arrives (pp. 84-85).

(7) There is no light matter relative to the precept of hearing Mass, in the sense that one may omit attendance one or the other time during the year (pp. 89-90).

(8) Those who have omitted parts of the Mass which constitute only light matter are obliged to supply the omissions (pp. 97-98).

(9) Heretics and schismatics, even those who have been born and reared outside the Catholic Church are obliged by the precept of hearing Mass (pp. 102-107).

(10) Excommunicates and those under interdict are obliged to attend Mass, when their censure merely deprives them of the right to assist at divine offices; they are obliged to remove the censure when it involves a prohibition from assisting at divine offices, if they can do so without moderately grave inconvenience (pp. 107-116).

(11) *"Sub dio"* must be interpreted to mean only "in the open air" and not "in any place whatsoever" (pp. 131-136).

(12) If a local ordinary grants permission for Mass to be celebrated outside of a church or oratory in order to enable a great number of the faithful to satisfy their obligation, all those whose necessity was the reason for the grant, can fulfill the precept in the place where the Mass is celebrated (pp. 137-141).

(13) The situations commonly existing in this country, such as the inability of a great number of the faithful to attend Mass on Sundays and Feastdays because of the limited capacity of the church, or because no church exists in the place, may be considered as "extraordinary cases" justifying the grant of permission to celebrate Mass outside of a church or oratory (pp. 143-145).

(14) *"Per modum actus"* must be strictly interpreted relative to the faculty of bishops to permit Mass outside of churches and oratories. In cases which will endure permanently or for a long period of time, the local ordinary should apply to the Holy See for a special indult (pp. 145-148).

(15) The distance necessary to constitute an excusing cause with regard to the precept of hearing Mass if an automobile can be used is about twenty miles, or as a more practical norm, a distance which would require a drive of an hour or more (pp. 159-160).

(16) For the lawful placing of a remote impediment to the precept of hearing Mass, or for the lawful non-removal of such an impediment, some inconvenience must *de facto* be involved (pp. 167-168).

(17) The local ordinary cannot dispense entire parishes from the precept of hearing Mass (pp. 171-173).

(18) The "individual case" in which local ordinaries and other competent persons can dispense from the precept of hearing Mass is determined by the cause warranting the dispensation (pp. 176-177).

BIBLIOGRAPHY

Sources

Acta Apostolicae Sedis, Commentarium Officiale, Romae, 1909—

Acta et Decreta Concilii Plenarii Baltimorensis Tertii, Baltimorae, 1886.

Acta et Decreta Sacrorum Conciliorum Recentiorum, Collectio Lacensis, 7 vols., Friburgi Brisgoviae, 1870-1892.

Bibliotheca Scriptorum Graecorum et Romanorum Teubneriana, ed. Müller, Leipzig, 1903.

Bullarii Romani Continuatio, 10 vols., Prati, 1843-1867.

Catechismus ex Decreto Concilii Tridentini ad Parochos Pii V. Pontificis Max. et deinde de Clementis XIII iussu editus, Romae, 1871.

Codex Iuris Canonici Pii X Pontificis Maximi iussu digestus Benedicti Papae XV auctoritate promulgatus, Romae: Typis Polyglottis Vaticanis, 1917.

Codicis Iuris Canonici Fontes cura Emi. Petri Card. Gasparri editi, 9 vols., Romae (postea Civitate Vaticana): Typis Polyglottis Vaticanis, 1923-1939. (Vols. VII, VIII, et IX ed. cura et studio Emi. Iustiniani Card. Serédi.)

Collectanea S. Congregationis de Propaganda Fide, 2 vols., Romae, 1907.

Concilii Plenarii Baltimorensis II. in Ecclesia Metropolitana Baltimorensi a die VII. ad diem XXI. Octobris, A.D. MDCCCLXVI., Habiti, et a Sede Apostolica recogniti, Acta et Decreta, editio altera, Baltimorae, 1894.

Corpus Iuris Canonici, ed. Lipsiensis 2. post Aemilii Ludovici Richter curas . . . instruxit Aemilius Friedberg, 2 vols., Lipsiae, 1879-1881.

Corpus Iuris Civilis, 3 vols., Vol. II *(Codex Iustinianus),* nova editio, ed. Krueger, Berolini: apud Weidmanos, 1915.

Corpus Scriptorum Ecclesiasticorum Latinorum, Vindobonae, 1866—

Decreta Authentica Congregationis Sacrorum Rituum ex actis eiusdem collecta eiusque auctoritate promulgata sub auspiciis SS. Domini Nostri Leonis Papae XIII, 6 vols., Romae: Typis Polyglottis Vaticanis, 1898-1927.

Denzinger, H.-Bannwart, C.-Umberg, I., *Enchiridion Symbolorum, Definitionum et Declarationum de Rebus Fidei et Morum,* 21.-23. ed., Friburgi Brisgoviae: Herder, 1937.

Florilegium Patristicum, digessit vertit adnotavit Gerardus Rauschen, 9 fasc., editio altera, Bonnae: Petri Hanstein, 1904-1913.

Funk, *Didascalia et Constitutiones Apostolorum,* 2 vols., Paderbornae, 1905.

Funk, *Patres Apostolici,* 2 vols., Tübingae, 1901.

Jaffé, Philippus, *Regesta Pontificum Romanorum ab condita ecclesia ad annum post Christum natum 1198,* editionem 2. correctam et auctam auspiciis Gulielmi Wattenbach curaverunt S. Loewenfeld, F. Kaltenbrunner, P. Ewald, 2 tomes in 1 vol., Lipsiae, 1885-1888.

Lightfoot, *The Apostolic Fathers,* London, 1898.

Mansi, Joannes, *Sacrorum Conciliorum Nova et Antiquissima Collectio,* 53 vols. in 59, Florentiae, Parisiis, Arnhem et Leipzig, 1901-1927.

Migne, Jacques P., *Patrologiae Cursus Completus, Series Graeca,* 161 vols., Parisiis, 1856-1866.

———, *Patrologiae Cursus Completus, Series Latina,* 221 vols., Parisiis, 1844-1864.

Monumenta Germaniae Historica, Legum Sectio II, Capitularia Regum Francorum, 2 tomes in 5 vols., ed. A. Boretius et V. Krause, Hannoverae, 1883-1897.

———, *Legum Sectio III, Concilia,* 2 tomes and 1 supplement, ed. F. Maassen, A. Werminghoff, H. Bastgen, Hannoverae et Lipsiae, 1883-1924.

Sacrosancti et Oecumenici Concilii Tridentini Canones et Decreta, Parisiis, 1832.

Reference Works

Aertnys, J.-Damen, C. A., *Theologia Moralis secundum doctrinam S. Alfonsi de Liguori,* 11 ed., 2 vols., Taurinorum Augustae: Marietti, 1928.

Alphonsus M. De Liguori, St., *Homo Apostolicus,* editio nova, ed. Saraceno, Taurini, 1890.

———, *Theologia Moralis,* ed. L. Gaudé, 4 vols., Romae, 1905-1912.

Andrews, John Nevins-Conrad, Ludwig Richard, *History of the Sabbath and the First Day of the Week,* 4. ed., Washington: Review and Herald Publ. Assn., 1912.

Antoninus, St., *Summa Sacrae Theologiae, Iuris Pontificii, et Caesarei,* 4 vols., Venetiis, 1571.

Augustine, P. Chas., *A Commentary on the New Code of Canon Law,* 8 vols., St. Louis: Herder, 1925-1938. Vol. IV, 3. ed., 1925; vol. VI, 3. ed., 1931.

Ayrinhac, H. A., *Administrative Legislation in the New Code of Canon Law,* New York: Longmans, Green & Co., 1930.

———, *Penal Legislation in the New Code of Canon Law,* New York: Benziger Bros., 1920.

Becanus, Martinus, *Analogia Veteris ac novi testamenti, in qua primum status veteris, deinde consensus, proportio et conspiratio illius cum novo explicatur,* Lovanii, 1775.

Beste, Udalricus, *Introductio in Codicem,* Collegeville, Minn.: St. John's Abbey Press, 1938.

Billuart, F. Chas., *Summa Sancti Thomae Hodiernis Academiarum Moribus Accomodata,* 9. ed., 8 tomes, Parisiis, 1746.

Blat, Albertus, *Commentarium Textus Codicis Iuris Canonici,* 5 vols. in 6, Romae: Collegio "Angelico," 1921-1927.

Bonacina, Martinus, *Sacrae Theologiae Compendium Absolutissimum,* ed. De Laval, Londini, 1634.

Bouscaren, T. Lincoln, *The Canon Law Digest,* 2 vols. and Supplement, Milwaukee: Bruce. 1934-1937-1941.

Bucceroni, J., *Commentarium de Censuris,* Romae, 1885.

Butler, Alban, *The Movable Feasts, Fasts and Other Annual Observances of the Catholic Church*, New York, no date given.

Butler, Alban-Thurston, Herbert, *The Lives of the Saints*, 12 vols., New York: P. J. Kenedy, 1925-1938.

Cavagnis, Felix, *Institutiones Iuris Publici Ecclesiae*, 4 ed., 3 vols., Romae: Desclée, Lefebvre et Soc., 1906.

Cappello, Felix, *Tractatus Canonico-Moralis de Censuris iuxta Codicem Iuris Canonici*, 2. ed., Taurinorum Augustae: Marietti, 1925.

———, *Tractatus Canonico-Moralis de Sacramentis*, 3 vols. in 6, Taurini: Marietti, 1932-1939. Vol. I, 3. ed., 1938; vol. II, pars I, 3. ed., 1938; vol. II, pars II, 1. ed., 1932; vol. II, pars III, 1935; vol. III, partes I et II, 4. ed., 1939.

Catholic Encyclopedia, The, 15 vols., index and 2 supplements, New York, 1907-1922.

Chelodi, Ioannes, *Ius De Personis iuxta Codicem Iuris Canonici*, e. ed., Tridenti: Libr. Edit. Tridentum, 1921.

Cicognani, Amleto Giovanni, *Canon Law* (authorized English version by J. O'Hara and F. Brennan), Philadelphia: Dolphin Press, 1934.

Cocchi, Guidus, *Commentarium in Codicem Iuris Canonici ad usus Scholarum*, 5 vols. in 8, Taurini-Romae: Marietti, 1922-1930.

Conran, Edw. James, *The Interdict*, The Catholic University of America Canon Law Studies, n. 56, Washington, D. C.: The Catholic University of America, 1930.

Coronata, Matthaeus Conte a, *De Locis et Temporibus Sacris*, Augustae Taurinorum: Marietti, 1922.

Cotter, A. C., *Theologia Fundamentalis*, Worcester: The Heffernan Press, 1940.

Craisson, D., *Manuale Totius Iuris Canonici*, 6. ed., 4 vols., Pictavii: Oudin Fratres, 1880.

D'Annibale, Jos., *Summula Theologiae Moralis*, 3. ed., 3 vols., Romae, 1888.

Davis, Henry, *Moral and Pastoral Theology*, 3. ed., 4 vols., New York: Sheed & Ward, 1938.

DeMeester, A., *Iuris Canonici et Iuris Canonico-Civilis Compendium*, Nova editio, 3 vols. in 4, Brugis: Desclée, 1921-1928.

Dictionary of Christian Antiquities, ed. Smith-Cheetham, 2 vols., London, 1875-1880.

Dictionnaire d'Archéologie Chrétienne et de Liturgie, 16 vols. (cont.), ed. Cabrol-Leclerq, Paris, 1924—

Dictionnaire de Théologie Catholique, 25 vols., ed. Vacant-Mangenot, Paris, 1903-1937.

Döllinger, J. J., *The First Age of Christianity*, 2 vols., London, 1877.

Duchesne, Msgr. L., *Christian Worship: Its Origin and Evolution*, 5. ed., trans. from the 3. French edition by M. L. McClure, London: Society for the Promotion of Christian Knowledge, 1927.

Ellard, Gerald, *Christian Life and Worship*, Milwaukee: Bruce Publishing Co., 1933.

Fanfani, Ludovicus I., *De Iure Parochorum ad normam Codicis Iuris Canonici,* ed. altera, Taurini-Romae: Marietti, 1936.

Feldhaus, Aloysius H., *Oratories,* The Catholic University of America Canon Law Studies, n. 42, Washington, D. C.: The Catholic University of America, 1927.

Fortescue, Adrian, *The Mass: A Study of the Roman Liturgy,* 2. ed., London: Longmans, Green & Co., 1926.

Franz, Adolph, *Die Messe im deutschen Mittelalter,* Freiburg im Breisgau: Herder, 1902.

Gasquet, Aidan, Abbe, *Parish Life in Medieval England,* New York: Benziger Bros., 1906.

Gasparri, Petrus, *Tractatus Canonicus de Sanctissima Eucharistia,* 2 vols., Parisiis: Delhomme et Briguet, 1897.

Gattico, Ioannes, *De Oratoriis Domesticis,* Romae, 1746.

Genicot-Salsmans, *Institutiones Theologiae Moralis,* 10. ed., 2 vols., Bruxellis: Alb. DeWit, 1922.

Gobat, George, *Experientiae Theologicae sive Experimentalis Theologia qua casibus prope septingentis factis non fictis explicatur in ordine ad praxim universa materia septem sacramentorum cum quadruplici indice,* Monachii, 1669.

Gury, Joannis P.-Ferreres, Joannes B., *Compendium Theologiae Moralis,* editio tertia Hispana, 2 vols., Barcinone: Subirana Fratres, 1906.

Herrmann, R. P., *Institutiones Theologiae Dogmaticae,* 6. ed., 2 vols., Lugdini: apud Emmanuelem Vitte, 1926.

Husslein, Joseph, *The Mass of the Apostles,* New York: P. J. Kenedy & Sons, 1929.

Hyland, Francis Edward, *Excommunication,* The Catholic University of America Canon Law Studies, n. 49, Washington, D. C.: The Catholic University of America, 1928.

Iorio, Thomas A., *Theologia Moralis iuxta methodum compendii Ioannis P. Gury, S.J., et Raphaelis Tummulo, S.J.,* 6. ed., 3 vols., Neapoli: M. D'Auria, 1938-1939.

Kellner, K. A. Heinrich, *Heortology: A History of the Christian Festivals from their origin to the present day,* trans. from 2. German edition, London: Kegan Paul, Trench, Trübner and Co., 1908.

Kenrick, Franciscus Patricius, *Theologia Moralis,* 3 vols., Philadelphiae, 1841-1843.

Kirchenlexikon, 12 vols., ed. Hergenröther-Kaulen, Freiburg im Breisgau, 1882-1901.

Konings, A., *Theologia Moralis Novissimi Ecclesiae Doctoris S. Alphonsi in Compendium Redacta, et usui venerabilis cleri Americani accommodata,* Bostoniae: Patricius Donahoe, 1874.

Konings-Putzer, *Commentarium in Facultates Apostolicas,* 4. ed., Neo-Eboraci: Benziger Fratres, 1897.

Lehmkuhl, Augustinus, *Theologia Moralis*, 9. ed., 2 vols., Friburgi Brisgoviae: Herder, 1898.

Lewis, A. H., *A Critical History of Sunday Legislation from 321 to 1888 A.D.*, New York, 1888.

———, *A Critical History of the Sabbath and the Sunday in the Christian Church*, New York, 1886.

Lexikon für Theologie und Kirche, 10 vols., Freiburg im Breisgau: Herder & Co., 1930-1938.

Many, S., *Praelectiones de Missa*, Parisiis, Letouzey et Ané, 1903.

Marc, Clement-Gestermann, Fr. X., *Institutiones Morales Alphonsianae*, 17. ed., 2 vols., Lugduni: Emmanuel Vitte, 1922.

Maringola, Aloysius, *Antiquitatum Christianarum Institutiones*, 2 vols. in 1, Neapoli, 1857.

Maroto, Philippus, *Institutiones Iuris Canonici ad Normam Novi Codicis*, 2 vols., 1919; Vol. I, 3. ed., 1921, Romae: Commentarium pro Religiosis.

Merkelbach, Benedictus Henricus, *Summa Theologiae Moralis ad mentem D. Thomae et ad Normam iuris novi*, 3. ed., 3 vols., Parisiis, Desclée de Brouwer et Soc., 1936-1939.

Michiels, P. Gomarrus, *Normae Generales Iuris Canonici*, 2 vols., Lublin, Polonia: Universitas Catholica, 1929.

Noldin, H.-Schmitt, A., *De Praeceptis Dei et Ecclesiae*, 25. ed., Oeniponte/Lipsiae: Feliciani Rauch, 1938.

———, *De Principiis*, 26. ed., Oeniponte/Lipsiae: Feliciani Rauch, 1939.

———, *De Sacramentis*, 19. ed., Oeniponte/Lipsiae: Feliciani Rauch, 1929.

Noldin, H.-Schönegger, *De Censuris*, 14.-15. ed., Oeniponte/Lipsiae: Feliciani Rauch, 1923.

Panzuti, Blasius, *Theologia Moralis*, 3. ed., 4 vols., Neapoli, 1840.

Paulus, C., *Welt- und Ordensklerus beim Ausgang des XIII. Jahrhunderts im Kampfe um die Pfarr-Rechte*, Essen-Ruhr, 1900.

Probst, Ferdinand, *Kirchliche Disciplin in den drei ersten christlichen Jahrhunderten*, Tübingen, 1873.

Prümmer, Dominicus M., *Manuale Iuris Canonici*, 4.-5. ed., Friburgi Brisgoviae: Herder & Co., 1927.

———, *Manuale Theologiae Moralis secundum Principia S. Thomae Aquinatis*, 8. ed., 3 vols., Friburgi Brisgoviae: Herder & Co., 1935-1936.

Raus, J. B., *Institutiones Canonicae iuxta novum codicem juris*, altera editio, Lugduni: Emmanuelis Vitte, 1931.

Reiffenstuel, Anacletus, *Ius Canonicum Universum*, 7 vols., Parisiis: 1864-1870.

Reilly, Edward M., *The General Norms of Dispensation*, The Catholic University of America Canon Law Studies, n. 119, Washington, D. C.: The Catholic University of America Press, 1939.

Rodgers, Edith Cooperrider, *Discussion of Holidays in the Later Middle Ages*, New York: Columbia University Press, 1940.

Roelker, Edward G., *Principles of Privilege according to the Code of Canon Law,* The Catholic University of America Canon Law Studies, n. 35, Washington, D. C.: The Catholic University of America, 1926.

Ruinart, P. Theodore, *Acta Martyrum,* Freiburg im Breisgau, 1802.

Sabetti-Barrett, *Compendium Theologiae Moralis,* 8. ed. post Codicem, Neo-Eboraci: Frederick Pustet Co., 1939.

Schumacher, H., *A. Handbook of Scripture Study,* 2. ed., 3 vols., St. Louis: Herder, 1924-1926.

Schürer, Emil, *Geschichte des Jüdischen Volkes im Zeitalter Jesu Christi,* 2. ed., 2 vols., Leipzig, 1886.

Sherry, Robert Joseph, *De Temporibus Sacris,* The Catholic University of America Canon Law Studies, Licentiate Dissertation (typewritten manuscript), Washington, D. C., 1923.

Sporer, Patricius, *Theologia Moralis super Decalogum,* 3. ed., Salisburgi, 1711.

Stapper, Richard-Baier, David, *Catholic Liturgics,* Paterson, N. J.: St. Anthony Guild Press, 1935.

Suarez, Franciscus, *Opera Omnia,* 28 vols., Parisiis: 1856-1878.

Tanquerey, Ad., *Synopsis Theologiae Moralis et Pastoralis,* 3 vols., Vols. I and III, 10. ed., Vol. II, 9. ed., Parisiis: Desclée, 1931.

Thomas Aquinas, St., *Summa Theologica,* 5 vols., Taurini: Marietti, 1928.

Thomas ex Charmes, *Theologia Universa,* 2. ed., Parisiis: Ludovicus Vives, 1862.

Thomassin, Louis, *Traité des Festes de l'Eglise,* Paris, 1683.

Van Hove, A., *De Legibus Ecclesiasticis,* Mechliniae: Dessain, 1930.

Vermeersch, A., *Theologiae Moralis Principia, Responsa, Concilia,* ed. altera, 3 vols., Brugis: Charles Bayaert, 1926-1928.

Vermeersch, A.-Creusen, J., *Epitome Iuris Canonici,* 3 vols., Vols. I et II, 5. ed., Vol. III, 4. ed., Mechliniae: Dessain, 1931-1934.

———, *Summa Novi Iuris Canonici,* 4. ed., Mechliniae: Dessain, 1921.

Villien, A., *A. History of the Commandments of the Church,* St. Louis: B. Herder, 1915.

Wernz, Franciscus X., *Ius Decretalium ad usum praelectionum in scholis textus canonici sive Iuris Decretalium,* ed. altera, 6 vols., Romae: Ex Typographia Polyglotta, 1905-1908.

Wernz, F. X.-Vidal, P., *Ius Canonicum,* 7 tomes in 8 vols., Romae: apud Aedes Universitatis Gregorianiae, 1923-1938.

Wilson, *History and Significance of the Lord's Day,* London, 1910.

Wouters, Ludovicus, *Manuale Theologiae Moralis,* 2 vols., Brugis (Belgii): Carolus Beyaert, 1932.

Woywod, Stanislaus, *A Practical Commentary on the Code of Canon Law,* 3. ed., 2 vols., New York: Wagner, 1929.

Zahn, Theodor, *Geschichte des Sonntags in der alten Kirche,* Hannover, 1878.

Periodicals

American Catholic Quarterly Review, The, 48 vols., Philadelphia, 1876-1923.

Clergy Review, The, London, 1931—

Ecclesiastical Review, The (originally *The American Ecclesiastical Review*), Philadelphia, 1889—

Periodica de Re Canonica et Morali utili praesertim Religiosis et Missionariis, Brugis, 1905—; ab anno 1927: *Periodica de Re Morali, Canonica, Liturgica.*

Theologisch-praktische Quartalschrift, Linz, 1832—

Articles

Barry, Alfred, "Lord's Day,"—*Dictionary of Christian Antiquities,* II, 1042-1053.

Bastnagel, Clement, "Assisting at Mass in the Parish Church,"—*ER,* CIV (1941), 463-467.

Bouscaren, Timotheus, "De Missa ex licentia Ordinarii celebrata . . ."—*Periodica,* XXVIII (1939), 52-61.

Dublanchy, E., "Dimanche,"—*Dictionnaire de Théologie Catholique,* Vol. IV, part II, cols. 1308-1348.

Dumaine, H., "Dimanche,"—*Dictionnaire d'Archéologie Chrétienne et de Liturgie,* Vol. IV, part I, cols. 858-994.

Haneburg, "Gottesdienst,"—*Kirchenlexikon,* V, 891-892.

Kuhn, Siegfried, "Sonntag,"—*Lexikon für Theologie und Kirche.*

McReavy, L. L., "Servile Work,"—*The Clergy Review,* IX (1935), 268-284.

Nevins, J., "Mass-Going and the Automobile,"—*ER,* LXXVIII (1928), 127-135.

Nötscher, Friedrich, "Sabbath,"—*Lexikon für Theologie und Kirche,* IX (1937), 48-50.

Shea, John Gilmary, "The Church and Her Holydays,"—*The American Catholic Quarterly Review,* XI (1886), 462-475.

Schmid, Franz, "Worin gründet die Pflicht der Sonntagsruhe,"—*Theologisch-praktische Quartalschrift,* LIII (1900), 12-26.

Anonymous, "Sunday Mass and the Parish Church,"—*ER,* XCVIII (1938), 459-465.

ABBREVIATIONS

AAS—*Acta Apostolicae Sedis.*
Bull. Rom. Continuatio—*Bullarii Romani Continuatio, ed. Prati.*
CLD—*Canon Law Digest* (Bouscaren).
Coll. Lac.—*Acta et Decreta Sacrorum Conciliorum Recentiorum, Collectio Lacensis.*
CSEL—*Corpus Scriptorum Ecclesiasticorum Latinorum.*
Coll. S.C.P.F.—*Collectanea S. Congregationis de Propaganda Fide,* ed. 1907.
Decr. Auth. S. R. C.—*Decreta Authentica Congregationis Sacrorum Rituum.*
ER—*The Ecclesiastical Review.*
Fontes—*Codicis Iuris Canonici Fontes.*
Mansi—*Sacrorum Conciliorum Nova et Antiquissima Collectio.*
MPG—Migne, *Patrologia, Series Graeca.*
MPL—Migne, *Patrologia, Series Latina.*
JK—Jaffé, *Regesta Pontificum Romanorum.*
MGH—*Monumenta Germaniae Historica.*
P. C. I.—*Pontificia Commissio Interpretationis.*
Periodica—*Periodica de Re Canonica et Morali Utili praesertim Religiosis et Missionariis.*

ALPHABETICAL INDEX

BIOGRAPHICAL NOTE

John Joseph Guiniven was born in the city of Philadelphia on May 23, 1911. He received his primary education in the parochial school of St. Boniface, from which he was graduated in June, 1925. After spending six years in the Redemptorist Preparatory College at North East, Pa., he entered the novitiate of the Redemptorist Congregation at Ilchester, Md., where he was professed on August 2, 1932. He then pursued his seminary studies at Mount St. Alphonsus, Esopus, N. Y., and was ordained to the Priesthood on June 20, 1937. In September, 1939, he was sent to the Catholic University of America, from which he received the Baccalaureate in Canon Law in June, 1940, and the Licentiate in June, 1941.

CANON LAW STUDIES

1. FRERIKS, REV. CELESTINE A., C.PP.S., J.C.D., Religious Congregations in Their External Relations, 121 pp., 1916.
2. GALLIHER, REV. DANIEL M., O.P., J.C.D., Canonical Elections, 117 pp., 1917.
3. BORKOWSKI, REV. AURELIUS L., O.F.M., J.C.D., De Confraternitatibus Ecclesiasticis, 136 pp., 1918.
4. CASTILLO, REV. CAYO, J.C.D., Disertacion Historico-Canonica sobre la Potestad del Cabildo en Sede Vacante o Impedida del Vicario Capitular, 99 pp., 1919 (1918).
5. KUBELBECK, REV. WILLIAM J., S.T.B., J.C.D., The Sacred Penitentiaria and Its Relation to Faculties of Ordinaries and Priests, 129 pp., 1918.
6. PETROVITS, REV. JOSEPH, J.C., S.T.D., J.C.D., The New Church Law on Matrimony, X-461 pp., 1919.
7. HICKEY, REV. JOHN J., S.T.B., J.C.D., Irregularities and Simple Impediments in the New Code of Canon Law, 100 pp., 1920.
8. KLEKOTKA, REV. PETER J., S.T.B., J.C.D., Diocesan Consultors, 179 pp., 1920.
9. WANENMACHER, REV. FRANCIS, J.C.D., The Evidence in Ecclesiastical Procedure Affecting the Marriage Bond, 1920 (Printed 1935).
10. GOLDEN, REV. HENRY FRANCIS, J.C.D., Parochial Benefices in the New Code, IV-119 pp., 1921 (Printed 1925).
11. KOUDELKA, REV. CHARLES J., J.C.D., Pastors, Their Rights and Duties According to the New Code of Canon Law, 211 pp., 1921.
12. MELO, REV. ANTONIUS, O.F.M., J.C.D., De Exemptione Regularium, X-188 pp., 1921.
13. SCHAAF, REV. VALENTINE THEODORE, O.F.M., S.T.B., J.C.D., The Cloister, X-180 pp., 1921.
14. BURKE, REV. THOMAS JOSEPH, S.T.D., J.C.D., Competence in Ecclesiastical Tribunals, IV-117 pp., 1922.
15. LEECH, REV. GEORGE LEO, J.C.D., A Comparative Study of the Constitution "Apostolicae Sedis" and the "Codex Juris Canonici," 179 pp., 1922.
16. MOTRY, REV. HUBERT LOUIS, S.T.D., J.C.D., Diocesan Faculties According to the Code of Canon Law, II-167 pp., 1922.
17. MURPHY, REV. GEORGE LAWRENCE, J.C.D., Delinquencies and Penalties in the Administration and the Reception of the Sacraments, IV-121 pp., 1923.
18. O'REILLY, REV. JOHN ANTHONY, S.T.B., J.C.D., Ecclesiastical Sepulture in the New Code of Canon Law, II-129 pp., 1923.
19. MICHALICKA, REV. WENCESLAS CYRILL, O.S.B., J.C.D., Judicial Procedure in Dismissal of Clerical Exempt Religious, 107 pp., 1923.

20. Dargin, Rev. Edward Vincent, S.T.B., J.C.D., Reserved Cases According to the Code of Canon Law, IV-103 pp., 1924.
21. Godfrey, Rev. John A., S.T.B., J.C.D., The Right of Patronage According to the Code of Canon Law, 153 pp., 1924.
22. Hagedorn, Rev. Francis Edward, J.C.D., General Legislation on Indulgences, II-154 pp., 1924.
23. King, Rev. James Ignatius, J.C.D., The Administration of the Sacraments to Dying Non-Catholics, V-141 pp., 1924.
24. Winslow, Rev. Francis Joseph, O.F.M., J.C.D., Vicars and Prefects Apostolic, IV-149 pp., 1924.
25. Correa, Rev. Jose Servelion, S.T.L., J.C.D., La Potestad Legislativa de la Iglesia Catolica, IV-127 pp., 1925.
26. Dugan, Rev. Henry Francis, A.M., J.C.D., The Judiciary Department of the Diocesan Curia, 87 pp., 1925.
27. Keller, Rev. Charles Frederick, S.T.B., J.C.D., Mass Stipends, 167 pp., 1925.
28. Paschang, Rev. John Linus, J.C.D., The Sacramentals According to the Code of Canon Law, 129 pp., 1925.
29. Piontek, Rev. Cyrillus, O.F.M., S.T.B., J.C.D., De Indulto Exclaustrationis necnon Saecularizationis, XIII-289 pp., 1925.
30. Kearney, Rev. Richard Joseph, S.T.B., J.C.D., Sponsors at Baptism According to the Code of Canon Law, IV-127 pp., 1925.
31. Bartlett, Rev. Chester Joseph, A.M., LL.B., J.C.D., The Tenure of Parochial Property in the United States of America, V-108 pp., 1926.
32. Kilker, Rev. Adrian Jerome, J.C.D., Extreme Unction, V-425 pp., 1926.
33. McCormick, Rev. Robert Emmett, J.C.D., Confessors of Religious, VIII-266 pp., 1926.
34. Miller, Rev. Newton Thomas, J.C.D., Founded Masses According to the Code of Canon Law, VII-93 pp., 1926.
35. Roelker, Rev. Edward G., S.T.D., J.C.D., Principles of Privilege According to the Code of Canon Law, XI-166 pp., 1926.
36. Bakalarczyk, Rev. Richardus, M.I.C., J.U.D., De Novitiatu, VIII-208 pp., 1927.
37. Pizzuti, Rev. Lawrence, O.F.M., J.U.L., De Parochis Religiosis, 1927. (Not Printed.)
38. Bliley, Rev. Nicholas Martin, O.S.B., J.C.D., Altars According to the Code of Canon Law, XIX-132 pp., 1927.
39. Brown, Mr. Brendan Francis, A.B., LL.M., J.U.D., The Canonical Juristic Personality with Special Reference to its Status in the United States of America, V-212 pp., 1927.
40. Cavanaugh, Rev. William Thomas, C.P., J.U.D., The Reservation of the Blessed Sacrament, VIII-101 pp., 1927.
41. Doheny, Rev. William J., C.S.C., A.B., J.U.D., Church Property: Modes of Acquisition, X-118 pp., 1927.

42. Feldhaus, Rev. Aloysius H., C.PP.S., J.C.D., Oratories, IX-141 pp., 1927.
43. Kelly, Rev. James Patrick, A.B., J.C.D., The Jurisdiction of the Simple Confessor, X-208 pp., 1927.
44. Neuberger, Rev. Nicholas J., J.C.D., Canon 6 or the Relation of the Codex Juris Canonici to the Preceding Legislation, V-95 pp., 1927.
45. O'Keefe, Rev. Gerald Michael, J.C.D., Matrimonial Dispensations, Powers of Bishops, Priests, and Confessors, VIII-232 pp., 1927.
46. Quigley, Rev. Joseph A. M., A.B., J.C.D., Condemned Societies, 139 pp., 1927.
47. Zaplotnik, Rev. Johannes Leo, J.C.D., De Vicariis Foraneis, X-142 pp., 1927.
48. Duskie, Rev. John Aloysius, A.B., J.C.D., The Canonical Status of the Orientals in the United States, VIII-196 pp., 1928.
49. Hyland, Rev. Francis Edward, J.C.D., Excommunciation, Its Nature, Historical Development and Effects, VIII-181 pp., 1928.
50. Reinmann, Rev. Gerald Joseph, O.M.C., J.C.D., The Third Order Secular of Saint Francis, 201 pp., 1928.
51. Schenk, Rev. Francis J., J.C.D., The Matrimonial Impediments of Mixed Religion and Disparity of Cult, XVI-318 pp., 1929.
52. Coady, Rev. John Joseph, S.T.D., J.U.D., A.M., The Appointment of Pastors, VIII-150 pp., 1929.
53. Kay, Rev. Thomas Henry, J.C.D., Competence in Matrimonial Procedure, VIII-164 pp., 1929.
54. Turner, Rev. Sidney Joseph, C.P., J.U.D., The Vow of Poverty, XLIX-217 pp., 1929.
55. Kearney, Rev. Raymond A., A.B., S.T.D., J.C.D., The Principles of Delegation, VII-149 pp., 1929.
56. Conran, Rev. Edward James, A.B., J.C.D., The Interdict, V-163 pp., 1930.
57. O'Neill, Rev. William H., J.C.D., Papal Rescripts of Favor, VII-218 pp., 1930.
58. Bastnagel, Rev. Clement Vincent, J.U.D., The Appointment of Parochial Adjutants and Assistants, XV-257 pp., 1930.
59. Ferry, Rev. William A., A.B., J.C.D., Stole Fees, V-136 pp., 1930.
60. Costello, Rev. John Michael, A.B., J.C.D., Domicile and Quasi-Domicile, VII-201 pp., 1930.
61. Kremer, Rev. Michael Nicholas, A.B., S.T.B., J.C.D., Church Support in the United States, VI-136 pp., 1930.
62. Angulo, Rev. Luis, C.M., J.C.D., Legislation de la Iglesia sobre la intencion en la application de la Santa Misa, VII-104 pp., 1931.
63. Frey, Rev. Wolfgang Norbert, O.S.B., A.B., J.C.D., The Act of Religious Profession, VIII-174 pp., 1931.
64. Roberts, Rev. James Brendan, A.B., J.C.D., The Banns of Marriage, XIV-140 pp., 1931.

65. Ryder, Rev. Raymond Aloysius, A.B., J.C.D., Simony, IX-151 pp., 1931.
66. Campagna, Rev. Angelo, Ph.D., J.U.D., Il Vicario Generale del Vescovo, VII-205 pp., 1931.
67. Cox, Rev. Joseph Godfrey, A.B., J.C.D., The Administration of Seminaries, VI-124 pp., 1931.
68. Gregory, Rev. Donald J., J.U.D., The Pauline Privilege, XV-165 pp., 1931.
69. Donohue, Rev. John F., J.C.D., The Impediment of Crime, VII-110 pp., 1931.
70. Dooley, Rev. Eugene A., O.M.I., J.C.D., Church Law on Sacred Relics, IX-143 pp., 1931.
71. Orth, Rev. Clement Raymond, O.M.C., J.C.D., The Approbation of Religious Institutes, 171 pp., 1931.
72. Pernicone, Rev. Joseph M., A.B., J.C.D., The Ecclesiastical Prohibition of Books, XII-267 pp., 1932.
73. Clinton, Rev. Connell, A.B., J.C.D., The Paschal Precept, IX-108 pp., 1932.
74. Donnelly, Rev. Francis B., A.M., S.T.L., J.C.D., The Diocesan Synod, VIII-125 pp., 1932.
75. Torrente, Rev. Camilo, C.M.F., J.C.D., Las Processiones Sagradas, V-145 pp., 1932.
76. Murphy, Rev. Edwin J., C.PP.S., J.C.D., Suspension Ex Informata Conscientia, XI-122 pp., 1932.
77. MacKenzie, Rev. Eric F., A.M., S.T.L., J.C.D., The Delict of Heresy in its Commission, Penalization, Absolution, VII-124 pp., 1932.
78. Lyons, Rev. Avitus E., S.T.B., J.C.D., The Collegiate Tribunal of First Instance, XI-147 pp., 1932.
79. Connolly, Rev. Thomas A., J.C.D., Appeals, XI-195 pp., 1932.
80. Sangmeister, Rev. Joseph V., A.B., J.C.D., Force and Fear as Precluding Matrimonial Consent, V-211 pp., 1932.
81. Jaeger, Rev. Leo A., A.B., J.C.D., The Administration of Vacant and Quasi-Vacant Episcopal Sees in the United States, IX-229 pp., 1932.
82. Rimlinger, Rev. Herbert T., J.C.D., Error Invalidating Matrimonial Consent, VII-79 pp., 1932.
83. Barrett, Rev. John D. M., S.S., J.C.D., A Comparative Study of the Third Plenary Council of Baltimore and the Code, IX-221 pp., 1932.
84. Carberry, Rev. John J., Ph.D., S.T.D., J.C.D., The Juridical Form of Marriage, X-177 pp., 1934.
85. Dolan, Rev. John L., A.B., J.C.D., The Defensor Vinculi, XII-157 pp., 1934.
86. Hannan, Rev. Jerome D., A.M., S.T.D., LL.B., J.C.D., The Canon Law of Wills, IX-517 pp., 1934.
87. Lemieux, Rev. Delise A., A.M., J.C.D., The Sentence in Ecclesiastical Procedure, IX-131 pp., 1934.

88. O'Rourke, Rev. James J., A.B., J.C.D., Parish Registers, VII-109 pp., 1934.
89. Timlin, Rev. Bartholomew, O.F.M., A.M., J.C.D., Conditional Matrimonial Consent, X-381 pp., 1934.
90. Wahl, Rev. Francis X., A.B., J.C.D., The Matrimonial Impediments of Consanguinity and Affinity, VI-125 pp., 1934.
91. White, Rev. Robert J., A.B., LL.B., S.T.B., J.C.D., Canonical Ante-Nuptial Promises and the Civil Law, VI-152 pp., 1934.
92. Herrera, Rev. Antonio Parra, O.C.D., J.C.D., Legislacion Ecclesiastica sobra el Ayuno y la Abstinencia, XI-191 pp., 1935.
93. Kennedy, Rev. Edwin J., J.C.D., The Special Matrimonial Process in Cases of Evident Nullity, X-165 pp., 1935.
94. Manning, Rev. John J., A.B., J.C.D., Presumption of Law in Matrimonial Procedure, XI-111 pp., 1935.
95. Moeder, Rev. John M., J.C.D., The Proper Bishop for Ordination and Dimissorial Letters, VII-135 pp., 1935.
96. O'Mara, Rev. William A., A.B., J.C.D., Canonical Causes for Matrimonial Dispensations, IX-155 pp., 1935.
97. Reilly, Rev. Peter, J.C.D., Residence of Pastors, IX-81 pp., 1935.
98. Smith, Rev. Mariner T., O.P., S.T.Lr., J.C.D., The Penal Law for Religious, VII-169 pp., 1935.
99. Whalen, Rev. Donald W., A.M., J.C.D., The Value of Testimonial Evidence in Matrimonial Procedure, XIII-297 pp., 1935.
100. Cleary, Rev. Joseph F., J.C.D., Canonical Limitations on the Alienation of Church Property, VIII-141 pp., 1936.
101. Glynn, Rev. John C., J.C.D., The Promoter of Justice, XX-337 pp., 1936.
102. Brennan, Rev. James H., S.S., M.A., S.T.B., J.C.D., The Simple Convalidation of Marriage, VI-135 pp., 1937.
103. Brunini, Rev. Joseph Bernard, J.C.D., The Clerical Obligations of Canons 139 and 142, X-121 pp., 1937.
104. Connor, Rev. Maurice, A.B., J.C.D., The Administrative Removal of Pastors, VIII-159 pp., 1937.
105. Guilfoyle, Rev. Merlin Joseph, J.C.D., Custom, XI-144 pp., 1937.
106. Hughes, Rev. James Austin, A.B., A.M., J.C.D., Witnesses in Criminal Trials of Clerics, IX-140 pp., 1937.
107. Jansen, Rev. Raymond J., A.B., S.T.L., J.C.D., Canonical Provisions for Catechetical Instruction, VII-153 pp., 1937.
108. Kealy, Rev. John James, A.B., J.C.D., The Introductory Libellus in Church Court Procedure, XI-121 pp., 1937.
109. McManus, Rev. James Edward, C.SS.R., J.C.D., The Administration of Temporal Goods in Religious Institutes, XVI-196 pp., 1937.
110. Moriarty, Rev. Eugene James, J.C.D., Oaths in Ecclesiastical Courts, X-115 pp., 1937.

111. Rainer, Rev. Eligius George, C.SS.R., J.C.D., Suspension of Clerics, XVII-249 pp., 1937.
112. Reilly, Rev. Thomas F., C.SS.R., J.C.D., Visitation of Religious, VI-195 pp., 1938.
113. Moriarty, Rfv. Francis E., C.SS.R., J.C.D., The Extraordinary Absolution from Censures, XV-334 pp., 1938.
114. Connolly, Rev. Nicholas P., J.C.D., The Canonical Erection of Parishes, X-132 pp., 1938.
115. Donovan, Rev. James Joseph, J.C.D., The Pastor's Obligation in Prenuptial Investigation, XII-322 pp., 1938.
116. Harrigan, Rev. Robert J., M.A., S.T.B., J.C.D., The Radical Sanation of Invalid Marriages, VIII-208 pp., 1938.
117. Boffa, Rev. Conrad Humbert, J.C.D., Canonical Provisions for Catholic Schools, VII-211 pp., 1939.
118. Parsons, Rev. Anscar John, O.M.Cap., J.C.D., Canonical Elections, XII-236 pp., 1939.
119. Reilly, Rev. Edward Michael, A.B., J.C.D., The General Norms of Dispensation, XII-156 pp., 1939.
120. Ryan, Rev. Gerald Aloysius, A.B., J.C.D., Principles of Episcopal Jurisdiction, XII-172 pp., 1939.
121. Burton, Rev. Francis James, C.S.C., A.B., J.C.D., A Commentary on Canon 1125, X-222 pp., 1940.
122. Miaskiewicz, Rev. Francis Sigismund, J.C.D., Supplied Jurisdiction According to Canon 209, XII-340 pp., 1940.
123. Rice, Rev. Patrick William, A.B., J.C.D., Proof of Death in Prenuptial Investigation, VIII-156 pp., 1940.
124. Anglin, Rev. Thomas Francis, M.S., J.C.D., The Eucharistic Fast, VIII-183 pp., 1941.
125. Coleman, Rev. John Jerome, J.C.D., The Minister of Confirmation, VI-153 pp., 1941.
126. Downs, Rev. Joseph Emmanuel, A.B., J.C.D., The Concept of Clerical Immunity, XI-163 pp., 1941.
127. Esswein, Rev. Anthony Albert, J.C.D., Extrajudicial Penal Powers of Ecclesiastical Superiors, X-144 pp., 1941.
128. Farrell, Rev. Benjamin Francis, M.A., S.T.L., J.C.D., The Rights and Duties of the Local Ordinary Regarding Congregations of Women Religious of Pontifical Approval, V-195 pp., 1941.
129. Feeney, Rev. Thomas John, A.B., S.T.L., J.C.D., Restitutio in Integrum, VI-169 pp., 1941.
130. Findlay, Rev. Stephen William, O.S.B., A.B., J.C.D., Canonical Norms Governing the Deposition and Degradation of Clerics, XVII-279 pp., 1941.
131. Goodwine, Rev. John, A.B., S.T.L., J.C.D., The Right of the Church to Acquire Property, VIII-119 pp., 1941.

132. HESTON, REV. EDWARD LOUIS, C.S.C., Ph.D., S.T.D., J.C.D., The Alienation of Church Property in the United States, XII-222 pp., 1941.
133. HOGAN, REV. JAMES JOHN, A.B., S.T.L., J.C.D., Judicial Advocates and Procurators, XIII-200 pp., 1941.
134. KEALY, REV. THOMAS M., A.B., Litt.B., J.C.D., Dowry of Women Religious, IX-152 pp., 1941.
135. KEENE, REV. MICHAEL JAMES, O.S.B., J.C.D., Religious Ordinaries and Canon 198, V-164 pp., 1942.
136. KERIN, REV. CHARLES A., S.S., M.A., S.T.B., J.C.D., The Privation of Christian Burial, XVI-279 pp., 1941.
137. LOUIS, REV. WILLIAM FRANCIS, M.A., J.C.D., Diocesan Archives, X-101 pp., 1941.
138. MCDEVITT, REV. GILBERT JOSEPH, A.B., J.C.D., Legitimacy and Legitimation, X-247 pp., 1941.
139. MCDONOUGH, REV. THOMAS JOSEPH, A.B., J.C.D., Apostolic Administrators, X-217 pp., 1941.
140. MEIER, REV. CARL ANTHONY, A.B., J.C.D., Penal Administration Procedure Against Negligent Pastors, XI-240 pp., 1941.
141. SCHMIDT, REV. JOHN ROGG, A.B., J.C.D., The Principles of Authentic Interpretation in Canon 17 of the Code of Canon Law, XII-331 pp., 1941.
142. SLAFKOSKY, REV. ANDREW LEONARD, A.B., J.C.D., The Canonical Episcopal Visitation of the Diocese, X-197 pp., 1941.
143. SWOBODA, REV. INNOCENT ROBERT, O.F.M., J.C.D., Ignorance in Relation to the Imputability of Delicts, IX-271 pp., 1941.
144. DUBÉ, REV. ARTHUR JOSEPH, A.B., J.C.D., The General Principles for the Reckoning of Time in Canon Law, VIII-299 pp., 1941.
145. MCBRIDE, REV. JAMES T., A.B., J.C.D., Incardination and Excardination of Seculars, XX-585 pp., 1941.
146. KRÓL, REV. JOHN T., J.C.D., The Defendant in Ecclesiastical Trials, XII-207 pp., 1942.
147. COMYNS, REV. JOSEPH J., C.SS.R., A.B., J.C.D., Papal and Episcopal Administration of Church Property, XIV-155 pp., 1942.
148. BARRY, REV. GARRETT FRANCIS, O.M.I., J.C.L., Violation of the Cloister.
149. BOLDUC, REV. GATIEN, C.S.V., A.B., S.T.L., J.C.L., Les études dans les religions cléricales.
150. BOYLE, REV. DAVID JOHN, M.A., J.C.L., The Juridic Effects of Moral Certitude on Pre-Nuptial Guarantees.
151. CANAVAN, REV. WALTER JOSEPH, M.A., LITT.D., J.C.L., The Profession of Faith.
152. DESROCHERS, REV. BRUNO, A.B., PH.L., S.T.B., J.C.L., Le Premier Concile Plénier de Québec et le Code de Droit Canonique.
153. DILLON, REV. ROBERT EDWARD, A.B., J.C.L., Common Law Marriage.
154. DODWELL, REV. EDWARD JOHN, PH.D., S.T.B., J.C.L., The Time and Place for the Celebration of Marriage.

155. Donnellan, Rev. Thomas Andrew, A.B., J.C.L., The Obligation of the Missa pro Populo.
156. Eltz, Rev. Louis Anthony, A.B., J.C.L., Cooperators in Crimes According to Canon 2209.
157. Gass, Rev. Sylvester Francis, M.A., J.C.L., Ecclesiastical Pensions.
158. Guiniven, Rev. John Joseph, C.SS.R., J.C.L., The Precept of Hearing Mass.
159. Gulczynski, Rev. John Theophilus, J.C.L., The Desecration and Violation of Churches.
160. Hammill, Rev. John Leo, M.A., J.C.L., The Obligations of the Traveler According to Canon 14.
161. Haydt, Rev. John Joseph, A.B., J.C.L., Reserved Benefices.
162. Huser, Rev. Roger John, O.F.M., A.B., J.C.L., The Canonical Crime of Abortion.
163. Kearney, Rev. Francis Patrick, A.B., S.T.L., J.C.L., The Principles of Canon 1127.
164. Linahen, Rev. Leo James, S.T.L., J.C.L., De Absolutione Complicis In Peccato Turpi.
165. McCloskey, Rev. Joseph Aloysius, A.B., J.C.L., The Subject of Ecclesiastical Law According to Canon 12.
166. O'Neill, Rev. Francis Joseph, C.SS.R., J.C.L., The Dismissal of Religious in Temporary Vows.
167. Prince, Rev. John Edward, A.B., S.T.B., J.C.L., The Diocesan Chancellor.
168. Riesner, Rev. Albert Joseph, C.SS.R., J.C.L., Apostates and Fugitives from Religious Institutes.
169. Stenger, Rev. Joseph Bernard, J.C.L., The Mortgaging of Church Property.
170. Waldron, Rev. Joseph Francis, A.B., J.C.L., The Minister of Baptism.
171. Willett, Rev. Robert Albert, J.C.L., The Probative Value of Documents in Ecclesiastical Trials.
172. Woeber, Rev. Edward Martin, M.A., J.C.L., The Interpellations.

www.ingramcontent.com/pod-product-compliance
Lightning Source LLC
LaVergne TN
LVHW050238080826
844660LV00012B/550

* 9 7 8 0 8 1 3 2 2 3 4 7 6 *